Christopher Sinclair-Stevenson

A Touchstone Book
Published by Simon & Schuster Inc.
New York · London · Toronto · Sydney · Tokyo

'n France

DRAWINGS BY GLENN WOLFF

Touchstone
Simon & Schuster Building
Rockefeller Center
1230 Avenue of the Americas
New York, New York 10020

First Touchstone Edition 1989
TOUCHSTONE and colophon are registered
trademarks of Simon & Schuster Inc.
Designed by Edith Fowler
Manufactured in the United States of America

10 9 8 7 6 5 4 3 2 1
10 9 8 7 6 5 4 3 2 1 Pbk.

Library of Congress Cataloging in Publication Data

Sinclair-Stevenson, Christopher.
  When in France.

  Bibliography: p.
  Includes index.
  1. France—Civilization. 2. France—Description
and travel—1975– . 3. France—Social life and
customs—Miscellanea. 1. Title.
DC33.S54 1987 944.083′8 87-12844
ISBN 0-671-41644-8
ISBN 0-671-67564-8 Pbk.

Grateful acknowledgment is made to the following
for permission to reprint from previously published
materials:
  Century Hutchinson, Ltd., for Alan Houghton
Broderick's *Cross Channel.*
  Oxford University Press for Richard Cobb's
Promenades.
  Viking Penguin, Inc., for Elizabeth David's *An*
Omelette and a Glass of Wine.
  Alan and Jane Davidson for their translation of
Dumas on Food.
  A. D. Peters & Co. for Nicholas Faith's *The Wine-*
masters.
  Lescher & Lescher for M. F. K. Fisher's *Two*
Towns of the Provence.
  John Johnson, Ltd., for Alistair Horne's *The*
Price of Glory.
  Harry N. Abrams, Inc., for John Russell's *Paris.*
  Dr. Theodore Zeldin for *France 1848-1945.*

FOR DEB
AND FOR RICHARD SIMON

Contents

Preface

I FIRST CAME to France far too late. I was eighteen years old when I arrived at Calais, boarded the train to Paris, and prepared for the great expedition to Blois, where my schoolboy French was to be polished. Perhaps, though, it was the right age after all. If I had been going regularly as a child to the beaches of Brittany (the South of France would have been judged too hot and perhaps too exciting) I might have become blasé. As it was, the shock of the new at a most impressionable age was overwhelming. Just a few miles across the English Channel and into another world, more vivid, more seductive, a little unnerving, wonderfully different. Metaphorically at least, I lay down and let myself be seduced. I have been repeating the delicious process ever since. And, in this case, repetition has never diminished my very first thrill. It is this sense of discovery, this sense of excitement, which I have tried to convey in this brief book. I envy those readers who have yet to lose their soul to France. And I envy myself, because there is still so much of that country to investigate, to savor, to enjoy.

When in France is more evocation than analysis. It is not a work of scholarship or deep research. It is not intended to be. It is opinionated, and no doubt readers will disagree with the opinions. I have perhaps been harsh about examples of modern architecture, about the effects of tourism, about aspects of the French character. Opinions are only opinions; they are not pronouncements engraved on tablets of stone. I have written about the parts of France I know best—Provence, Paris, the Loire, the Channel ports—and I have inspected the characteristics of the French which most interest me. There is little here of economics, or education, or politics. There is some history, there is some social history, there is some topography.

The themes which I have chosen may appear arbitrary, and even inconclusive—ingredients failing to create, when mixed together, a satisfying dish. I have, though, attempted to design a logical path toward my finale. I start with the Channel and with Boulogne, where so many tourists have started; it is a first glimpse of France. Then, naturally, I move on to Paris, which many people consider *is* the quintessential France. After that come three lighthearted chapters on sex, food, and drink, in order to give, so to speak, a social base. The third geographical chapter, a tour of some of the châteaux of the Loire in the steps of Henry James, is sandwiched between short biographical essays on two very different, but in my view equally French, men. Henri IV seems all heart, but conceals exquisite sense and sensitivity; Voltaire seems all intellect, but was one of the most impassioned railers against injustice in the history of the modern world. They personify, between them, many of the most likable French characteristics.

The fourth geographical chapter concerns the South, and from there it is an easy step to the exotic lure of French overseas colonies. An analysis of the French concept of *"la gloire,"* which inspired such expansion, is the brighter face of the appalling degradation suffered by France during three catastrophic wars, when the iron could truly be said to have entered the French soul. And so, finally and inevitably, to a consideration of clichés and chauvinism, of how the French are seen and how they in turn view other nations.

IT WOULD be absurd to challenge Theodore Zeldin and his majestic work *France 1848–1945*; Richard Cobb's unique view of regions and people; J. G. Weightman's encyclopedic knowledge of French literature; Douglas Johnson's grasp of the history of modern France. My book is intended to give amusement and pleasure to readers who, through its pages, may be reminded of a place, or a quotation, or an impression. It is also a tribute to a country and a people I love, warts and all. As a publisher, I have been much influenced by Luigi Barzini's glorious book about his fellow countrymen. I have even tried, on occasion, to persuade writers to do for France what Barzini did for Italy. The results were not what I wanted, so I decided to do it myself—a case of appalling hubris. I am deeply grateful to *my* publishers in England and America for giving me that chance—even if nemesis strikes.

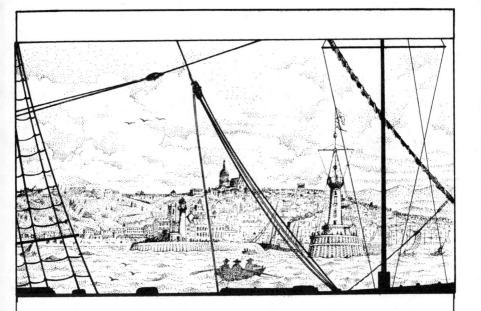

i

Cross-Channel

I N JUNE 1763, Dr. Tobias Smollett, "a surly Scotchman" but a munificent host to the Grub Street journalists, and author of two highly successful picaresque novels recording the fictional adventures of Roderick Random and Peregrine Pickle, caught his first sight of Boulogne, one of the traditional marine gateways to France. He had crossed the Channel in a Folkestone cutter, and it had been an uncomfortable journey. "The cabin was so small that a dog could hardly turn in it, and the beds put me in mind of the holes described in some catacombs, in which the bodies of the dead were deposited, being thrust in with the feet foremost; there was no getting into them but endways, and indeed they seemed so dirty, that nothing but extreme necessity could have obliged me to use them." He had sat up all night, the sea was rough, he was cold and cramped and weary.

It was an inauspicious start to his journey through France and on into Italy, but worse was to follow. The captain of the cutter could not enter Boulogne harbor because of the high wind, so Smollett and his entourage were consigned to the ship's boat. They had hardly left the cutter when they were met by a second boat coming from the shore. The Boulogne watermen were exercising their traditional, though no doubt illegal, right to carry ashore any visitor—at a price.

Smollett was forced to change boats in the middle of a choppy sea, and then to sit in a waterlogged boat while a packet of mail was fetched from the cutter. "We were afterwards rowed a long league, in a rough sea, against wind and tide, before we reached the harbour, where we landed, benumbed with cold, and the women excessively sick: from our landing-place we were obliged to walk very near a mile to the inn where we purposed to lodge, attended by six or seven men and women, bare-legged, carrying our baggage."

The boat cost him a guinea, and he had to tip every one of the bare-legged porters. He was still less amused when he realized that the whole affair was a conspiracy between the captain of the cutter and the Boulogne watermen. Future passengers, he thought, should be warned: "When a man hires a packet-boat from Dover to Calais or Boulogne, let him remember that the stated price is five guineas; and let him insist upon being carried into the harbour in the ship, without paying the least regard to the representations of the master, who is generally a little dirty knave." And they should also be warned about the appalling behavior of the French: "When we arrived at the inn, all the beds were occupied; so that we were obliged to sit in a cold kitchen above two hours, until some of the lodgers should get up. This was such a bad specimen of French accommodation, that my wife could not help regretting even the inns of Rochester, Sittingbourn, and Canterbury: bad as they are, they certainly have the advantage, when compared with the execrable auberges of this country, where one finds nothing but dirt and imposition. One would imagine the

French were still at war with the English, for they pillage them without mercy."

And so was born the complete Francophobe, a character often met in diaries and novels, and indeed in real life. What Smollett failed to realize was that the inhabitants of the Channel ports are businessmen rather than enemies.

Boulogne and Calais, for so many people, British and American, in the pre-jet age, were the twin entrances into Europe. There were, of course, in addition Cherbourg and Saint-Malo, Dieppe and Dunkirk, but these were somehow different, mildly eccentric choices. Boulogne and Calais were the real thing, and they still are. Much has, inevitably, changed. These days, with most holiday-makers' insatiable need to get from one place to another as fast as possible, and with the building of the vast Paris airport complex at Charles de Gaulle, a futuristic maze of conveyor belts and radial tunnels, the small pleasures of arriving in France by sea are limited to the impecunious student, the family with a car, and the occasional traveler who prefers trains to planes. No doubt when the Channel Tunnel is finally built (and one feels that, after so many delays and arguments, it never will, or should, be built), the roads of Brittany and Normandy will be packed end to end, but for the moment a certain calm still reigns.

The cross-Channel boats are bigger now, for the convenience of the internal combustion engine en masse. First-class sections have vanished, though the tickets often promise them, and Mr. James Sherwood, the American who has reintroduced the splendors of the Orient Express, assures us that they will be restored on his boats. The stewards look quite anonymous. Long gone are the faded green leather seats, the offers of comforting pots of tea and buttered toast, the ready availability of porters. Gone, too, is one particular steward, sporting a peculiarly unbecoming ginger wig, who seemed to be ever-present like some gnomelike Flying Dutchman. Instead, there is inescapable pop music, a total absence of edible food (except on the French boats), sweaty young men in Union Jack shorts, and mammoth consumption of duty-free beer.

But many of the pleasures do remain, particularly when you have avoided the summer. Julian Barnes put it well in *Flaubert's Parrot:* "I like these out-of-season crossings. When you're young you prefer the vulgar months, the fullness of seasons. As you grow older you learn to like the in-between times, the months that can't make up their minds." The looming clock tower of Calais is still there, hideous but reassuring. The gaggle of blue-denimed porters, cheap cigarettes hanging from their lower lips, wait to pounce. There are the mingled smells of garlic, Gitanes, and urine which seem to ooze from the walls; the uniforms of the gendarmes and the *douaniers;* the trains waiting beyond the customs shed. The customs officials seem more relaxed than at Dover or Folkestone, as Smollett discovered back in the middle of the eighteenth century: "I brought no plate along with me, but a dozen and a half of spoons, and a dozen teaspoons: the first being found in one of our portmanteaus, when they were examined at the bureau, cost me seventeen livres *entrée;* the others being luckily in my servant's pocket, escaped duty free."

The trains themselves are duller, the compartments seem more cramped, the Bar Grill Express, self-service with too few tables at Ritz prices, though undeniably hugely superior to any British or American counterpart, has superseded the old dining cars with their pink lampshades and *café-filtre* which never seemed to filter and the certainty of sitting opposite a femme fatale. The Flèche d'Or—it sounded even better, more seductive than the Golden Arrow—actually had movable, though massive, armchairs at each table, and a chef perfectly capable of crowning a five-course lunch with exquisite *crêpes Normande.* The Train Bleu was more splendid still, since it progressed in a leisurely way along that strange no-man's-line between the Gare du Nord and the Gare de Lyon, before setting out at *l'heure du dîner* for the pine-scented Midi. And there were the connections for Amsterdam and Munich and Copenhagen, and for the Simplon-Orient Express to Venice and Trieste.

Like much else, French trains are not what they used to be. The admirable Mistral, which left Paris at lunchtime and cruised down through Lyons and the Rhône valley and on to Marseilles and the Riviera, has been abandoned. The double-decker commuter trains impress, because they look so odd, and the *trains à grande vitesse* (TGV for short) impress because they are fast and efficient. But a prepacked cold meal tasting mainly of vinegar is a poor substitute for an excellent lunch in the wagon-restaurant. Indeed, sensible French travelers have begun to boycott the meals on the TGV's, and the SNCF is being forced to restore the old haute cuisine. They have made a start on the Paris–Strasbourg line, and further improvements are keenly anticipated.

But there is still the excitement of inspecting the notice boards on the side of each carriage—Bâle, Roma, Messina, München, Hamburg—and knowing that you will wake up on the other side of Europe. Even the route to Paris has its well-remembered sights: the hovercraft station at Boulogne, the miniature château almost on the railway line, the small country stations encrimsoned with roses and geraniums, the lines of poplars, the flashing streams, the signal-box *postes* as the metropolis looms, the sight of the Sacré-Coeur floodlit against the Paris sky. You are in France, and a strange mingling of relaxation and anticipation takes over.

The traveler always seems to feel that he must hurtle on, leaving the scudding clouds of the Channel as if they might carry him back to England. This is a mistake. Dieppe, Calais, and Boulogne have much to offer. There are the people, so different in their more direct northern way, an apparent calm superimposed on a layer of excitability, even of violence. And there are the towns themselves. Calais is perhaps the least appealing, partly because it was so appallingly damaged during the Second World War, though it has excellent restaurants and shops. Dieppe has considerable charm and a firmly based reputation for a particularly rich style of cooking; a *garniture dieppoise*—a mixture of mussels, prawns, white wine, and a velouté sauce—has become part of the language. Dieppe has also always been a great favorite of the English. In the nineteenth century, gentlefolk in reduced circumstances and gamblers escaping their creditors settled happily there until their fortunes were restored; there were no less than eleven schools expressly for English young ladies.

Boulogne is both more substantial and more of a piece than either Calais or Dieppe. Tobias Smollett, though he disapproved of so much, did have a few polite words for the high standard of food available.

> The beef is neither fat nor firm; but very good for soup, which is the only use the French make of it. The veal is not so white, nor so well fed, as the English veal; but it is more juicy, and better tasted. The mutton and pork are very good. We buy our poultry alive, and fatten them at home. Here are excellent turkies, and no want of game: the hares, in particular, are very large, juicy, and high-flavoured. The best part of the

fish caught on this coast is sent post to Paris, in *chasse-marines,*
by a company of contractors, like those of Hastings in Sussex.
Nevertheless, we have excellent soles, skaite, flounders and
whitings, and sometimes mackarel. The oysters are very large,
coarse, and rank.

But the sour old Scot could not resist adding a disagreeable footnote: "Notwithstanding all the haste the contractors can make,
their fish in the summer is very often spoiled before it arrives at
Paris . . . At best it must be in such a mortified condition, that
no other people, except the negroes on the coast of Guinea, would
feed upon it."

And on the subject of wine, Smollett had decided views:

The wine commonly drunk at Boulogne comes from Auxerre,
is very small and meagre, and may be had from five to eight
sols a bottle; that is, from twopence halfpenny to fourpence.
The French inhabitants drink no good wine; nor is there any
to be had, unless you have recourse to the British wine merchants here established, who deal in Bourdeaux wines,
brought hither by sea for the London market. . . . I don't
believe there is a drop of generous Burgundy in the place;
and the aubergistes impose upon us shamefully, when they
charge it at two livres a bottle. . . . All the brandy which I
have seen in Boulogne is new, fiery, and still-burnt. This is
the trash which the smugglers import into England.

Two hundred and twenty-four years later, the visitor would
have no trouble in finding good brandy. But therein lies a problem. Boulogne has become a paradise for shoppers. Here they
come, a densely packed horde, determined of foot yet oddly vac-
uous of face. They have an air of avid desperation as they march
up the ramp to the harbor, dragging strange wheeled contraptions
behind them. They do not seem prepared for enjoyment, though
there is the faintest glint of expectation in the odd eye. They are
sensibly dressed and shod. They have no need of passports; frontiers do not exist for the day-tripper. They have come to shop.

If you stroll down Boulogne's Grande Rue—having perhaps
emerged from Lugand's reinforced by a rabidly strong coffee and
an irresistible chocolate calorie mountain—down toward the quai,
you will catch your first glimpse of this strange new breed of traveler. Outside Boulogne there is a giant supermarket, and it is to
that mecca they turn. Boulogne has many delights to offer: Phi-

lippe Olivier's *fromagerie,* a brace of first-class restaurants, a delightful walled Old Town replete with well-restored seventeenth-and eighteenth-century buildings, an absurdly grandiose cathedral, a museum devoted to Napoleonic *trouvailles* brought back from the First Consul's Egyptian enterprise, a colorful marketplace. None of these, unfortunately (some would say fortunately), make any impression on the shoppers. For them it is bread not circuses: baguettes, liters of wine whose grape content may be somewhat suspect, pâtés and cheese, above all—eccentrically—beer, beer in very large quantities.

To be fair, the Boulonnais have no objection to this endless treasure trove of hard cash, and very efficiently they organize the acres of shelves and the buses which connect the supermarket with the ferries. It is the French who have become a nation of shopkeepers. And surely it must be mere rumor that they, in turn, sail to Dover and Folkestone to do their shopping. What can the attraction be? English beer?

In any case, Boulogne hardly suffers from these incursions. For a brief period, the cafés and cheaper fish restaurants on the quai fill up, but soon the tourists are all gone to the supermarket, and thence to the ferry, intent on consuming as much duty-free alcohol on board as they can before the grille of the bar comes crashing down outside Dover. The Boulonnais heave a sigh of relief, count the takings, and call for a pastis or a *fine à l'eau.* Boulogne has been given back to the Boulonnais.

And what of the Boulonnais themselves? Smollett was unimpressed, reserving his particular disgust for the nobility. Since he was writing a mere quarter of a century before the outbreak of the French Revolution, his words have a certain unconscious irony:

> I know not a more insignificant set of mortals than the noblesse of Boulogne; helpless in themselves, and useless to the community; without dignity, sense, or sentiment; contemptible from pride, and ridiculous from inanity. They pretend to be jealous of their rank, and will entertain no correspondence with the merchants, whom they term plebeians. They likewise keep at a great distance from strangers, on pretence of a delicacy in the article of punctilio: but, as I am informed, this statelieness is in a great measure affected, in order to conceal their poverty.

Warming to his theme, Smollett excoriated the sheer stupidity of the Boulogne *noblesse*.

> They have not the common sense to reside at their houses in the country, where, by farming their own grounds, they might live at a small expence, and improve their estates at the same time. They allow their country houses to go to decay, and their gardens and fields to waste; and reside in dark holes in the Upper Town of Boulogne without light, air, or convenience. There they starve within doors, that they may have wherewithal to purchase fine cloaths, and appear once a day in the church, or on the rampart. They have no education, no taste for reading, no housewifery, nor indeed any earthly occupation, but that of dressing their hair, and adorning their bodies. They hate walking, and would never go abroad, if they were not stimulated by the vanity of being seen. I ought to except indeed [and here is the sting in the tail, since Smollett makes no bones about his dislike of the Roman Catholic religion] those who turn devotees, and spend the greatest part of their time with the priest, either at church or in their own houses.

There seems, though, to have been precious little seriousness in devotional matters. "The only profane diversions of this place are a puppet-show and a mountebank; but then their religion affords a perpetual comedy. Their high masses, their feasts, their processions, their pilgrimages, confessions, images, tapers, robes, incense, benedictions, spectacles, representations, and innumerable ceremonies, which revolve almost incessantly, furnish a variety of entertainment from one end of the year to the other." Smollett is enjoying himself quite as much as the supposed Christians whom he mocks:

> A Roman catholic longs as impatiently for the festival of St Suaire, or St Croix, or St Veronique, as a schoolboy in England for the representation of punch and the devil; and there is generally as much laughing at one farce as at the other. Even when the descent from the cross is acted, in the holy week, with all the circumstances that ought naturally to inspire the gravest sentiments, if you cast your eyes among the multitude that croud the place, you will not discover one melancholy face: all is prattling, tittering, or laughing; and ten to one but you perceive a number of them employed in hissing the female who personates the Virgin Mary.

Now Roman Catholic churches are certainly more free and easy, and indeed more theatrical, than straitlaced Protestant, let alone Presbyterian, ones. The cathedral in Boulogne possesses a certain comic quality. The floral decorations are, more likely than not, faintly withered gladioli, a mixture of puce and virulent yellow, like so many elongated bruises. There are a variety of strange mementos dotted about the side aisles. The pièce de résistance is a most peculiar chariot which, for no very good reason, was dragged around northern France during the last war. It has the aspect of a meeting of minds between Canova and Salvador Dali, but is without doubt a relic of considerable local importance and sanctity, so one should not pour scorn.

The *noblesse* of Boulogne, if Smollett's description is in any way accurate, received their just deserts in 1789. In the twentieth century it is difficult to conceive of Boulogne possessing a *noblesse* at all. It seems a very middle class, a very bourgeois place in the real sense of the word. Léon Blum once maintained that "despite all appearances to the contrary, it is the bourgeoisie which has ruled France for the past century and a half," in other words since the Revolution. And, though "bourgeois" has become almost a term of abuse, the true bourgeois—the professional men, doctors, lawyers, and teachers, but also bankers and industrialists—maintain their hold on French society. Boulogne, like Rouen or Caen or any other sizable town you care to choose in the north of France, has probably not altered, in essence, since the days of Flaubert.

But one should not become too serious or sociological about Boulogne. It is certainly hard to do so if you stand on the end of the jetty. If you look inland, you see a pleasant seaside town, with no great pretensions but an abundance of delights, few of them flashy or meretricious: layers of houses rising up to the old walled town, the marketplace injecting an atmosphere of barter and commerce twice a week, the steep streets and rampart promenades preserving a touch of the crinoline and the frock coat. If you gaze out to sea, you are as likely as not to confront banked clouds massing over the Channel, the cumulus configurations which Boudin and Sickert painted. The light is seldom crystal-sharp, the sky rarely a crude, boring blue. There are always variation and novelty. You think of Debussy's "Rondes de Printemps" or "Ce qu'a vu le Vent de l'Ouest." You could almost be in England. But you are not. The voices of the day-trippers confuse for a second, but it is a transitory disturbance. La Manche could be a hundred or a thousand miles wide, the differences between the two sides of the Channel are so obvious. The first step on French soil, however many times it has been taken, always provides a new shock.

It also provides the essential breathing space, so that you can adapt yourself to the sheer pleasure of being in France. There is a sense of anticipation as you board the train, and as the seascape becomes the countryside. It is the train for Paris. The French businessmen bury themselves in their evening papers or the contents of their briefcases. There is no need to look out the windows. But you are a tourist. There may be problems of language and acclimatization ahead, but that heady feeling of irresponsibility is uppermost. The acidulous Smollett is forgotten. Next stop: Paris.

ii

Ville Lumière

AND NOW since it is the 'green hour'—since it is five
o'clock—let us take a chair outside the Café de la Paix
and watch the people pass, and meditate, here, in
the centre of the civilised world, on this wonderful
city of Paris and this wonderful country of France." Edward V.
Lucas was writing in 1909; *plus ça change* . . . Other cafés—
the Deux Magots, La Coupole, the Dôme—would become fashionable between the wars and after the war (and then there was Le
Drugstore), and their prices would rise and their atmosphere take
on a period element, as if the ghosts of Sartre or Camus or Hem-

ingway were still stirring the motes of dust, the dust of existentialism or of resistance or merely of rebellion.

One cannot imagine that there was ever much rebellion brewing in the Café de la Paix. For here is the comfortable, self-regarding nineteenth-century Paris of Haussmann,* of galas at the Opéra, of louche women in long cloaks seemingly in perpetual imitation of Camille (before the onset of consumption, of course), of smart carriages bowling up the Boulevard des Capucines or the Rue de la Paix, the Paris of *luxe, calme, et volupté.* Inside the Café de la Paix all is green and gold; cupids and nymphs frolic overhead; mysterious women in black pass through, looking but rarely finding. Occasionally the strains of an incongruous jazz band can be heard, conjuring up the brittle spirit of Noël Coward's Parisian Pierrot. On the pavement, oysters are being opened with a quick flash of the *huitrier's* knife, the plates of *belons* and *palourdes* whisked away, the smell of seaweed, lemon juice, and saltwater for a second defeating the diesel fumes.

The waiters deserve close attention (there are also, and increasingly, waitresses, but they are more reserved). They are, inevitably, characters. E. V. Lucas expatiated on the phenomenon of the Paris waiter, and what he said before the First World War still holds good for both sides of the Channel.

> Paris may be a city of feminine charm and domination; but to the ordinary foreigner, and especially the Englishman, it is far more a city of waiters. Women we have in England too; but waiters we have not. There are waiters in London, no doubt, but that is the end of them: there are, to all intents and purposes, no waiters in the provinces, where we eat exclusively in our own houses.† And even in London we must brace ourselves to find such waiters as there are: we must indulge in heroic feats of patience, and, once the waiter comes into view, exercise most of the vocal organs to attract his notice and obtain his suffrages. In other words, there is in London perhaps one waiter to every five thousand persons;

* *Baron Haussmann redesigned Paris during the Second Empire (1852–70). His changes were quite as drastic as those wrought by London's Great Fire.*

† *It must be admitted that there are now many waiters in the provinces of the British Isles. They are rarely British by birth. The British no longer approve of service, if indeed they ever did. Americans, on the other hand, approve strongly of service—or appear to—though the effect is mechanical rather than heartfelt.*

whereas in Paris there are five thousand waiters, more or less, to every one person. Or so it seems. It is a city of waiters; it is *the* city of waiters!

It cannot be pretended that the Café de la Paix is a mecca for gourmets. The food is not particularly good—are they incapable of making a passable omelette?—and far too large a proportion of the menu is given over to bizarre confections involving ice creams of improbable flavors, liqueurs of preposterous hues, and lavish whirls of whipped cream. That is not the point. One does not drop in at the Café de la Paix in search of gastronomic delights, it is the atmosphere that counts. And the atmosphere is very powerful: an amalgam of the enticing and the tawdry, the glossy green and gold concealing the cracks in the nineteenth-century opulence.

Perhaps it is more a Tower of Babel than a café. Certainly every language under the sun can be heard here: Midwest American, Japanese, Scandinavian, Spanish—the linguistic cornucopia overflows. Even French, very occasionally, breaks through. Single ladies in reduced circumstances sit over their coffee or *porto*, exchanging a desultory word with a skittering waitress. Couples drift in after the opera, firmly demanding a *kir royal*. A civil servant abandons the contents of his briefcase and decides that half a dozen oysters will stay the pangs of hunger until dinner. Everything is bustle, *va et vient*.

THE PLACE de la Bastille is a dreary circle, offering a metro station, a column, and a whiff of revolution. It is a pity that Napoleon's plan for a massive elephant fountain in the center of the Place was never carried out; that at least would have added a touch of crazed grandeur. To the west lies the Rue Saint-Antoine and the Marais; to the east runs the Rue du Faubourg Saint-Antoine, stretching interminably to the Place de la Nation.

It is a curious area, in the past frequently given to violence and insurrection, but also celebrated for its open-air entertainments. Above all, though, it has long been and still remains the cabinetmakers' district. Most of the finest examples of furniture and interior decoration emerged from the shops and ateliers of the Faubourg Saint-Antoine during the eighteenth century. Every expensive whim was catered for, from wallpaper to looking glasses, from automata to dog kennels.

The age of elegance is no more. Vulgarity is rife. The Rue du Faubourg Saint-Antoine now resembles something more akin to an Oriental bazaar. Windows display immense sofas in white leather, chairs apparently confected from onyx horns, tables of hideous pink alabaster and gilt. There is much imitation boule, bright and deceptive as a new-minted nickel coin. There is not a straight line in sight, everything is curlicues and extravagance. Half the world's animal population seems to have rendered up its skins and hides to be stretched over furniture of such amplitude that it must be designed for a race of vast-buttocked potentates. Here is a temptation of Saint Anthony which would have amazed even Hieronymus Bosch.

Such overwrought opulence cries out for a counterbalance, and to the west of the Place de la Bastille it exists in a most perfect form. John Russell vividly points the contrast: "The Bastille is to the Marais as Marseilles is to Aix-en-Provence, raw meat to rillettes, blowlamp to vesta." Only a few yards away from the memorial to Revolutionary Paris and you are in the Paris of

Henri IV. It is a small, concentrated area, the Marais, bordered by the Rue Saint-Antoine and the Rue de Bretagne to the south and north respectively, by the Rue du Temple on the west, and by the Rue de Turenne on the east. Once it was the most fashionable district in the whole of Paris, until the beginning of the eighteenth century, when the aristocrats moved further west to the Faubourg Saint-Germain, those that is who were not permanently at Versailles.

During the nineteenth century the Marais fell into a kind of slumber, like Perrault's Belle au Bois Dormant, decaying genteelly and then more precipitately. Before the First World War, a scheme was announced which would renovate what Haussmann had left of the old Paris at the huge cost of £52 million. Other considerations, military and economic, intervened, and it was not until well after the Second World War that the task of reconstruction and redecoration moved into top gear. Slowly, the great palaces and *hôtels* and embassies emerged from their grimy carapaces. The Hôtel Lamoignon—where Mme de Sévigné and Boileau talked in the seventeenth century and Alphonse Daudet entertained Flaubert, Turgenev, Zola, and the Goncourts in the nineteenth—has been handed over to the Bibliothèque Historique de la Ville de Paris. The Hôtel Carnavalet, where Mme de Sévigné lived in the 1670s, is a museum, and the Hôtel de Soubise and the Hôtel de Rohan have become the Archives Nationales. But the Hôtel des Ambassadeurs de Hollande, with its magnificent courtyard and its memories of Mme du Deffand and of Beaumarchais, is still privately owned.

The Marais is steeped in history. As E. V. Lucas says, "Wherever one enters one finds the traces of splendour, intrigue and romance; howsoever modern conditions may have robbed them of their glory, to walk in these streets is, for anyone with any imagination, to recreate Dumas." It is a fair point. The Man in the Iron Mask was incarcerated a stone's throw away in the Bastille (the mask was of velvet not metal); in a narrow passage off the Rue des Francs-Bourgeois Charles VI's brother, Louis, Duc d'Orléans, was killed in November 1407 by Jean le Hardi, Duc de Bourgogne; on the central balcony of the Hôtel de Beauvais in the Rue François-Miron, Anne of Austria and Cardinal Mazarin waited for the triumphal entry into Paris of Louis XIV and his queen Marie-Thérèse.

And then there is the Place des Vosges. Once it was called the Place Royale, appropriately since it was Henri IV who commissioned its construction and whose own pavilion was built over the gateway which separates the Place itself from the Rue de Birague. Before then, it was the courtyard of the Palais des Tournelles in which Gabriel de Montgomery, Captain of the Scotch Guard, accidentally killed Henri II during a tournament. Montgomery, for his pains, was executed in the Place de l'Hôtel-de-Ville, and Catherine de Medici razed the Palais des Tournelles. Henri IV rescued it from its ignominy as a horse market, and set his seal on the most beautiful square in Paris.

Richelieu's *hôtel* was there, and a famous duel was fought in front of it. One almost expects d'Artagnan and the Three Musketeers to come swaggering out of one of those superb doorways, plumed hats at a challenging tilt and swords itching to be drawn from their scabbards. It is hardly surprising that Rachel, the great tragic actress, lived in the Place des Vosges. (Perhaps she would approve of the fact that the Marais became a strongly Jewish area.) Here, too, lived Victor Hugo.

Some critics dislike the Place des Vosges almost because of its perfection. The sheer openness of the Place and the height of the houses contradict, it is true, the hugger-mugger narrowness and compression of the Marais as a whole. But those glorious red and white houses of stone and brick with their high-sloping roofs and oeil-de-boeuf windows have a majesty which wholly compensates for the rather dingy garden in the middle. In an aerial photograph the green square looks all of a piece with the surrounding buildings; at ground level, the statue of Louis XIII, removed during the Revolution and restored in 1825, has a mild incongruity, surrounded as it is by shrieking children rushing across the gravel toward a second-rate adventure playground. Perhaps it needs fountains, perhaps it needs nothing but grass. Perhaps perfection is impossible.

OPINIONS ARE divided on the subject of the enclosed park and galleries of the Palais Royal. Here is E. V. Lucas:

> That strange white and green oasis into which it is so simple never to stray. When I first knew Paris the Palais Royal was filled with cheap restaurants and shops to allure the excur-

sionist and the connoisseur of those books which an inspired catalogue once described as very curious and disgusting. It is now practically deserted; the restaurants have gone and few shops remain; but in the summer the band plays to happy crowds, and children frolic here all day. I have, however, never succeeded in shaking off a feeling of depression.

And here is John Russell:

All persons of good character like the Palais Royal. Nowhere is Paris more quiet, for one thing. Not Venice itself is more free from wheeled traffic, the windows overlooking the garden are unimpeachably private, and although there are shops in plenty beneath the arcades, the traffic within them is of a secretive and all but soundless character. Out of school hours the garden has an occasional wild animation, but on the whole the atmosphere suggests a rather grand almshouse or home for convalescents of distinction. Spectatorship is the main local activity; and Colette, one of its finest practitioners, once kept a whole book afloat with what she could see from her window above the Palais Royal gardens.

There is indeed an air of great calm about the arcades and gardens of the Palais Royal. There are children—and why not, since there are two shops at the Rue de Beaujolais end of the gardens, one a general toyshop, the other specializing in all manner of musical boxes and clocks and anything else that can be induced mechanically to play a tune, which would entrance any child. There are—a sign of the times—joggers, but decorous ones in pairs, watched with some disdain by the cat in the window of the musical box emporium. There are civil servants hastening to their favorite café or restaurant. But there are few tourists, few shoppers, mainly because the shops along the arcades under those fine lanterns do not beckon to the usual run of impulse buyer. Few foreigners would feel impelled to enter one of the many shops selling blazingly gaudy campaign medals and obscure orders once presented by European and South American monarchs and presidents to deserving or no doubt often thoroughly undeserving generals and ambassadors. Stamps issued by French colonial administrations and old theater posters and necklaces made of semiprecious stones, rose quartz, lapis lazuli, and tourmaline, these are for the specialist. And the shops never seem to be open in any case

The many ghosts who frequent the Palais Royal remember rowdier times. Cardinal Richelieu, who built the original palace long before the three-sided addition, creating the present great courtyard, designed for the Duc de Chartres in the 1780s, favored noisy practical jokes. The Regent, the Duc d'Orléans, so admired and despaired of by Saint-Simon, found relaxation in a somewhat different manner. Saint-Simon himself recorded something of Philippe d'Orléans's dissolute behavior and the debauched style of life in the Palais Royal.

> After the Regency Council, or about five o'clock if there were no meeting, he was done with work. Now was his time for the Opéra or the Luxembourg, if he did not go there before his chocolate. Sometimes he visited Mme la Duchesse d'Orléans and occasionally supped with her. At other times he went out by the back offices, or had people admitted that way. . . . At home he ate his suppers in shocking bad company, with his mistresses or girls from the Opéra, often with Mme la Duchesse de Berry [his daughter, with whom, so rumor had it, he was conducting an incestuous affair] and some dozen young men, not always the same, whom he invariably spoke of as his *roués*. . . . At these suppers everyone was discussed, ministers and friends alike, with a licence that knew no bounds. The past and present love-affairs of the Court and Paris were examined without regard for the victims' feelings; old scandals were retold, ancient jests and absurdities revived, nothing and nobody was sacred. . . . The wine flowed, the company became heated; they talked filth and outrivalled one another in blasphemy; and when they had made sufficient noise and were all dead drunk, they were put to bed, and on the following day began all over again.

But it was when the Palais Royal was expanded into its present-day quadrilateral that licentiousness and then revolutionary fervor reached fever pitch. On 12 July 1789, one Camille Desmoulins leapt onto a table in the Café de Foy. He had come from Versailles with news of Louis XVI's dismissal of Necker, the chief minister and the only man thought capable of saving France from bankruptcy. Desmoulins found himself addressing a huge crowd. He seized his opportunity. He spoke of another St. Bartholomew's Day Massacre, he said that the Swiss Guard would be mobilized, with orders "to cut our throats to a man," he preached rebellion masquerading as self-defense.

Thomas Carlyle, in one of his grandest passages, teetering on the edge of absurdity, conjures up the scene.

> But see Camille Desmoulins, from the Café de Foy, rushing out, sibylline in face; his hair streaming, in each hand a pistol! He springs to a table: the Police satellites are eyeing him; alive they shall not take him, not they alive him alive. This time he speaks without stammering:—Friends! shall we die like hunted hares? Like sheep hounded into their pinfold; bleating for mercy, where is no mercy, but only a whetted knife? The hour is come; the supreme hour of Frenchman and Man; when Oppressors are to try conclusions with Oppressed; and the word is, swift Death, or Deliverance forever. Let such hour be *well*-come! Us, meseems, one cry only befits: To Arms! Let universal Paris, universal France, as with the throat of the whirlwind, sound only: To arms—To arms! yell responsive the unnumberable voices; like one great voice, as of a Demon yelling from the air: for all faces wax fire-eyed, all hearts burn up into madness. In such, or fitter words, does Camille evoke the Elemental Powers, in this great moment. —Friends, continues Camille, some rallying-sign! Cockades; green ones;—the colour of Hope!—As with the flight of locusts, these green tree-leaves; green ribands from the neighbouring shops; all green things are snatched, and made cockades of. Camille descends from his table, "stifled with embraces, wetted with tears"; has a bit of green riband handed him; sticks it in his hat. And now to Curtius' Image-shop there; to the Boulevards; to the four winds; and rest not till France be on fire!

The French Revolution had started, there among the trees of the Palais Royal. But when the Terror and the guillotining of the King and Queen had receded into the stuff of nightmares, the arcades returned to their old business. Louis Léopold Boilly's 1809 picture "The Galleries of the Palais Royal" shows a number of young women, lightly clad in the Empire style, their breasts barely half covered, being ogled or propositioned by some very determined men. One gentleman, wearing a frock coat, a top hat, and a leer, is actually encircling one of the girls with his arms, while she lifts her skirt to reveal a considerable amount of leg. A bargain is about to be struck. There is a seller of dogs and a seller of flowers. But the most interesting section of the painting is in the right-hand foreground. Here we see a girl who looks a trifle more respectable, perhaps because she is wearing a bonnet, perhaps because she is casting a sentimental eye à la Greuze on a pet rabbit being carried by a one-legged boy. Unfortunately, this pretty cameo is spoiled by three additions to the scene: a bejeweled black duenna (to put it politely); an Arab with a lascivious smile and a mustache; and, attached to the pillar, a sheet of paper bearing the words *"Avis aux Sexes."* No wonder the boy with the rabbit looks distinctly apprehensive.

That the Palais Royal had become, in effect, a permanent outdoor brothel is borne out in Galignani's *Paris Guide of 1822,* which refers to *"chevaliers d'industrie,* and Ladies equally industrious." In those days, there were large numbers of cafés and rooms of a more equivocal nature downstairs below the pavement. John Russell quotes a directory of 1804 which lists seventeen billiard saloons, eighteen gaming houses and—a nice, but inevitable, touch—eleven usurers. But by the end of the nineteenth century, partly because of so much destruction at the time of the Commune and partly because fashion and venereal transaction had moved westward, the Palais Royal was as E. V. Lucas saw it.

Today, though, it is a marvelous oasis, impeccably kept, best seen on a glittering spring day or when those trees which the followers of Camille Desmoulins plundered almost two centuries ago have taken on the russets and pale golds of autumn. Voices are not raised here; and in the early morning or late in the evening only the occasional footstep resounds down the arcades. A distant laugh is heard, an echo of Philippe d'Orléans's all-night parties? It is more likely to come from the Grand Véfour, a once-great restaurant now undergoing something of a reincarnation. It was a café in pre-Revolutionary days. Perhaps it was there that the painter Fragonard ate the final fatal ice cream that killed him. Now it is haute cuisine. Let John Russell have the last word: "It's not a place to drop into for a sandwich, but if you should happen to be invited there you can reflect between mouthfuls of *Toast aux Crevettes Rothschild* and *Lamproie Bordelaise* that Lamartine, Thiers, Sainte-Beuve, MacMahon, the Duc d'Aumale, Cocteau, and Colette may each and all, at one time or another, have sat where you sit."

The Palais Royal does indeed have its ghosts.

It WAS a very peculiar spectacle. Up the narrow street came a procession of weirdly dressed human beings, some in full medieval fig with long gowns and curious headgear, like a chorus line from a provincial production of *Die Meistersinger,* some more Renaissance in doublet and hose, the majority in ethnic costumes. The procession moved falteringly, as there was evidently a bottleneck up at the top of the street. During each halt, the groups dissolved into small pieces of theater, a cross between commedia dell'arte and a somewhat hesitant pageant. The hill was alive with music, which veered from comparative sweetness to abject cacophony. Tortured notes emerged from wind instruments of extravagant shape: pipes, tabors, bagpipes, cornets. There was a great deal of drumming, always a safe standby. There were a number of diminutive children, apparently imitating American football cheerleaders, high-stepping, baton-twirling, courageous, and sadly uncoordinated.

We pushed on up into the Place du Tertre, hoping to find some clues as to what all this overexcited street show was about. And then we realized. It was, of course, being the autumn, a celebration of the *vendange,* the harvesting of the wine grapes. For each little group obviously represented a particular part of France producing some sort of wine. The banners held proudly aloft proclaimed the names of Bergerac and Provence, of Alsace and Burgundy, of Chinon and Cahors.

Most European cities indulge in similar celebrations at special times of the year. I have often witnessed the spring festival in Zurich, when the guilds dress up in their carefully preserved tabards and breeches and cloaks, march through the town, and come to a halt outside the old opera house, when they proceed to charge on their horses round and round an enormous snowman, now being consumed in an impressive conflagration to mark the ritual ending of winter. Siena has the Palio, Spain her running of the bulls, England her beating the bounds. But the procession that autumn day up the steep streets of Montmartre had a most charming uniqueness. It was disorganized and rather out at elbows (even the crack French cavalry regiments reveal on Bastille Day that

pageantry is not a Gallic forte), many of the participants had all too clearly lunched satisfactorily, the music and the marching were only distantly related, and there were signs that membership of this particular brouhaha was not exactly select: a few flourishes from Normandy spoke in praise of the apple rather than the grape. Nevertheless, everyone had entered into the spirit of the occasion with such gusto that it was impossible not to smile indulgently.

And Montmartre, in any case, has such a raffishness and vulgarity that even the oddest addition is safely absorbed. The Place du Tertre, the center of all the bustle, may invoke memories in some of Henri Murger's *Vie de Bohème* or Charpentier's *Louise,* and in the early morning, before the crowds have come, it is fresh and pretty and above all picturesque. By the afternoon, when it is packed with tourists and deplorably bad itinerant artists and narcoticized students and pickpockets, it resembles more a small, claustrophobic hell. The restaurants are overpriced and mediocre, the so-called antique shops are optimistic with their dating, the galleries display as great a quantity of rubbish as could be gathered together in such a small area.

And yet, and yet . . . On a sharp spring day, when the leaves on the plane trees are an almost acid green, when the Square Willette is occupied only by a few old women in rusty black resting after their shopping expedition, when the smell of newly baked bread wafts insinuatingly up the Rue Steinkerque, then Montmartre reclaims itself. Even the pavement artists look less raddled, and their work can be forgiven as bright rather than gaudy. And the view is stupendous, down over the roofs of Paris to the serpentine Seine, across to the Buttes-Chaumont, a great sweep of domes and towers and pinnacles.

But there is a further problem. If you turn around from this amazing panorama, you cannot avoid the Sacré-Coeur. When this eccentric church was under construction in the first decade of this century, visitors had mixed feelings. E. V. Lucas was in considerable doubt.

> As for the cathedral [it is only a mere church, of course], that seems to me to be better seen and appreciated from the distance: from the train as one enters Paris in the late afternoon, with the level sun lighting its pure walls; from the heights on the south side of the river; from the Boulevard des Italiens up the Rue Laffitte; and from the Buttes-Chaumont. For the cathedral itself is not particularly attractive near at hand, and within it is cold and dull and still awaiting its glass. It was, however, one of the happiest thoughts that had come to Rome in our time to set this fascinating bizarre Oriental building here. It gave Paris a new note that it will now never lose.

A new note indeed, though I doubt whether it is a mellifluous one. Lucas is right that it should be seen from the train. Just before the Gare du Nord, there is a splendid sideways view of the basilica, lit and therefore whiter than a soap-powder advertisement. And it must be admitted that the Parisians do love this odd excrescence with its elongated cupolas. Dorothy Menpes, writing in exactly the same year as E. V. Lucas, thought much better of the interior and also remarked on the very large congregation.

> As one enters the church, the grand notes of the organ greet one's ears, and there is a heavy odour of incense mingled with that of lilies. The church is dim and dark and rich in colour; lofty. It is filled with people, most of them kneeling, but some wandering irreverently about the church. Everywhere is the gleam and glitter of candles and of brass and gold. The cen-

tral altar is a shining mass of golden points of light. All one
can see of the priest officiating is a huge green cross on a white
ground at his back. By the side of him kneels a boy in scarlet,
who crosses himself, and at intervals murmurs prayers. Suddenly the music stops; most of the candles are put out; only
the priest stays behind. The great doors of the church are
opened by two sisters with large white-winged caps; the light
of day is let in, the brilliant yellow sunshine; beyond the steps
one catches a glimpse of grey, distant, panoramic Paris.

It is a rich church, but it is a poor district. The tourist shops,
the nightclubs, the neon lights of the Boulevard de Clichy, the
ever-open doors promising unattainable dreams and staccato satisfaction, all this is the tawdry, fly-blown icing on a cake which
lacks richness and succulence. The Cimetière de Montmartre is
a better indicator than the pictures of Utrillo or shaky memories
of a *vie bohème* lived by whores who were always pretty and innocent even when they were dying of tuberculosis and by poets and
painters who were dashing and handsome and one day, one day,
would be famous. E. V. Lucas has a more chilling glimpse of the
real Montmartre as it was and perhaps still is.

I attended early mass at the Sacré-Coeur church on January 1, 1908. It was snowing lightly and very cold, and as I
came away, at about eight, and descended the hill towards
Paris, I was struck by the spectacle of the lame and blind and
miserable men and women who were appearing mysteriously
from nowhere to descend the hill too, groping and hobbling
down the slippery steepnesses. . . . I still tremble a little as I
remember the importunities of the Montmartre cripple of
ferocious aspect and no legs at all, fixed into a packing-case
on wheels, who, having demanded alms in vain, hurls himself
night after night along the pavement after the hard-hearted,
urging his torso's chariot by powerful strokes of his huge
hands on the pavement, as though he rowed against Leander,
with such menacing fury that I for one have literally taken to
my heels.

LUCAS'S BEGGARS had nowhere to go. In our modern age of un-
employment, the clochards and the down-and-outs have the metro.
The passageways have been given over to beggars from Algeria

and Equatorial Africa and the Middle East, and during the abnormally cold January weather at the beginning of 1985, permission was given to the penniless and homeless to sleep on the metro platforms.

The metro does, of course, have more basic uses. And it is one of the glories of Paris and a tribute to French ingenuity and style. The French are sensible about trains and rail transport. The *trains à grande vitesse* make British Rail or Amtrak appear antediluvian. Who else but the French would have invested millions of francs on new tracks and new trains?

And who else but the French would have exercised so much thought on the sheer design of the Paris metro station? Some of the trains may still be a trifle antiquated with their two classes of compartments (does anyone ever buy a first-class ticket?), their wooden seats, and their notices on the inadvisability of spitting and the absolute necessity of giving up one's seat to a *mutilé de guerre* or a pregnant woman. But the stations—or most of them—are marvels with their brightly colored and comfortable seats, their clean tiled walls, and every now and then a little picture show or a case of *objets* or, as in the Louvre station, a veritable slice of museum.

The metro system is clean, it is attractive, and it is easily comprehensible—qualities sadly lacking in both London's underground and New York's subway (New York is filthy, dangerous, but understandable; London is filthy, a little less dangerous, and baffling). Providing you are on the right line, you cannot go wrong. In addition, you are presented with an unending range of stations with curious or romantic or euphonious names. Forgotten politicians are resurrected. How many people remember that Alexandre-Auguste Ledru-Rollin was a member of the 1848 provisional government and a supporter of universal suffrage? There he is, between the Bastille and Faidherbe-Chaligny (according to Larousse, Louis Faidherbe organized *habilement* the colony of Senegal, commanded the Army of the North during the Franco-Prussian War, and became Grand Chancellor of the Légion d'Honneur; Antoine Chaligny was a craftsman in bronze at Louis XIV's court). Jean Jaurès, not unreasonably, finds himself near Simon Bolivar; and Charles de Gaulle, George V, Franklin Roosevelt, and Clemenceau are on a direct, peaceful line to Concorde. There are battles, many forgotten by everyone except French military historians: Campo Formio, Wagram, Pyramides, Alma. There are writers: Dumas, Victor Hugo, Voltaire, Malesherbes, Anatole France. Robespierre is far out in Montreuil, and Pierre Curie in Ivry (Marie, his wife, does not appear to merit a station—an early example of male discrimination?). More religious associations are provided by Saint Francis Xavier and the Filles du Calvaire; and there are a few dull-sounding stops like Convention, Volontaires, and Maubert-Mutualité (offset, though, by Gaîté, Plaisance, and Place des Fêtes). And who could resist the fragrant Jasmin and Porte des Lilas? The London telephone directory once had its pleasures, its exchanges such as Frobisher, Elgar, and Primrose, but its underground stations do not commemorate playwrights or composers. New York, quite properly in the circumstances, is wholly practical in the naming of subway stops.

THERE ARE two totally conflicting views on the Centre National d'Art Contemporain Georges Pompidou, or Beaubourg for short. Some say that it is a miracle of exciting architecture and color, a truly modern creation, just as the Eiffel Tower was a truly modern creation in the 1880s. Others denounce it as a monument of tawdry kitsch. It was designed over a period of seven years by Renzo Piano and Richard Rogers, the latter something of a guru to the supporters of the new brutalism in architecture. It did not, one must admit, cause a great deal of destruction of existing buildings, and it can be claimed that its creation in that dead area between the Boulevard de Sébastopol and the Marais has actually led to the admirable re-emergence of the Marais as one of the most beautiful parts of Paris, and moreover lived in. Equally, because of the existence of Beaubourg, a number of perfectly attractive apartment buildings have gone up nearby; pedestrian precincts have been allocated; and there is much liveliness and noise and light.

The fact that the church of Saint-Merri looks extremely incongruous, and that the fountains are a perfect center for touts and drug pushers, should not be laid at the door of Signor Piano and Mr. Rogers. Large open areas well provided with restaurants and nightclubs will never be given over to the pursuit of virtue and purity whether they are in New York, London, or Paris. There is, certainly, a shoddiness and seediness about the area, and the pedestrianized streets and squares sometimes resemble the last refuge of the international hippie. But all this is beside the point. Does the Centre Pompidou work? John Russell is in no doubt: "It is also held against Beaubourg that it works. This is not to say that it is a model of technical efficiency or inconspicuous hard wearing. Beaubourg was not built in expectation of anything like the degree of popular success that it has actually had, and it has naturally had its problems on that account. But Beaubourg works, in as much as it makes the arts accessible all the way across the board to a huge miscellaneous public. It also makes thought and discussion accessible on a scale that was formerly the privilege of a few."

In other words, the concept is to be applauded. The arts can mix freely; there is space; Beaubourg is not for a small elite of stuffy critics and experts, it is for everyone. "It is an inquisitive, impatient, improvisatory turn of mind. People flick from room to room at Beaubourg the way they flick from channel to channel on a television set." The simile is an apt one. It is indeed almost impossible to concentrate on one exhibition or one happening at the Centre Pompidou. To use that word so beloved of sociologists, it is all very unstructured.

So, too, are the actual buildings. Clive James has summed up the effect brilliantly: "The general idea of the building is that it wears its insides out. All the internal conduits are featured externally, arousing the fear that anything one contributes to the sewage system might reappear elsewhere in the building labelled as a work of art." The plethora of pipes and scaffolding poles and moving staircases make one think of an unfinished airport. (Charles de Gaulle airport is not dissimilar in effect, but it is finished and looks it.) In the bright sunshine, it does possess a kind of manic radiance. After a good meal, one is dazzled and delighted. On a gray day, it looks terrible, all that hectic gay modernism reduced to a series of messy children's construction sets.

Perhaps any attempt at a new style of architecture is doomed to critical disaster. No doubt Haussmann's heavy creations evoked cries of horror from the purists harking back to the eighteenth century; in turn, his grand vistas were spoiled by hideous blocks, like those of La Défense, rearing up in the distance. Certainly those extraordinary housing complexes which have been rising outside Paris and which resemble Greek temples have come in for bitter attack. Piano and Rogers are certainly not neo-classicists; they cannot be accused of imitation or adaptation. The Centre Pompidou at least has the courage of its own convictions, and it is a far superior creation to the dreadful Barbican Centre in London (though greatly inferior to many of the modern museums and art galleries in the United States, such as the Guggenheim or the Museum of Modern Art in New York). It has been the site of many imaginatively conceived exhibitions and musical events. But I wish that all those pipes had been left on the inside.

SOONER OR LATER, something has to be said about the Champs-Elysées. Once perhaps the fields were truly Elysian, but any heavenly connotation has long since fled. The lower end, running up from the Place de la Concorde, can be seen as more or less an extension of the Tuileries Gardens. Although the right-hand side is dwarfed by the regrettable Grand Palais, heavily Victorian and pompous, the left-hand section contains a pretty garden where well-brought-up children play decorously, a small theater, and some attractive views of the Elysée Palace and the American and British embassics. But from the Rond-Point des Champs-Elysées, where the Avenue Franklin D. Roosevelt and the Avenue Montaigne meet, all is lost until a certain serenity, dull though it may be, arrives with the great avenues stretching out beyond the Arc de Triomphe.

The Champs-Elysées are a disaster simply because they might be anywhere. There is nothing recognizably French or Parisian about this conglomeration of shops, boutiques, and arcades. It is as if London's King's Road, Tottenham Court Road, and a bit of Oxford Street had been placed in a giant imitation chrome cocktail shaker with a dash of West Forty-second Street and a touch of the least attractive part of Lexington Avenue. The mixture appears to have absorbed the ingredients, but the result tastes only of metal. Among the mess of cinemas and hamburger bars and car showrooms there is only one relic of a more Parisian age (there was until recently a second, but the Hotel Claridge has fallen to the developers), Fouquet's. It is both café and restaurant, the food is old-fashioned and therefore good, the waiters wear long white aprons and are marvelously deft as they glide between the tables. Fouquet's is patronized by businessmen, by ladies after a visit to the salons, by courtly old gentlemen in Prince of Wales checks. Fouquet's knows its place.

So instead of trekking on up the Champs-Elysées, it is best to lunch at Fouquet's, then stroll down the Avenue George V to the Pont d'Alma, then along the Seine by the Cours Albert 1er and the Cours La Reine, where Massenet's Manon sang her brightest aria and which until all too recently was quite as notorious for easy vice as the Palais Royal ever was. Just beyond the Grand Palais lies the Pont Alexandre III, the richest and most impressive bridge in Paris. At night, when all its globe lanterns are lit, it is magical. During the day, it is grand in an imperial way, with its gilded figures and caryatids. In the summer, the bridge and the Place des Invalides over the Seine seem about to burst into flames. But it is the right way to approach the Hôtel des Invalides.

First Louis XIV, then Napoleon. In both parts, *la gloire* is palpably present. The Sun King, in bas relief, caracoles on his horse on the main façade. It was he who commissioned the original military hospital, much as his cousin Charles II asked Christopher

Wren to design the Royal Hospital in Chelsea. Once it housed seven thousand wounded soldiers behind that exquisite seventeenth-century front. Now that function has disappeared, and the Musée de l'Armée has taken the place of all those *mutilés de guerre*. The whole ensemble reeks of military triumph and military disaster. The interior of Mansart's beautiful chapel is hung about with frayed colors, though these are in the main memorials to little, bloody, and vicious colonial wars, rather than to the great victories of Louis XIV or Napoleon. It is all very grand and sad and slightly hollow, like all memorials to man's destruction of his fellow man.

Then Napoleon. His figure dominates the Cour d'Honneur, and his body lies in its sarcophagus in a marble well; it was brought back to Paris in 1840, nineteen years after his death on Saint Helena. The sarcophagus is simple and severe. And over the entrance to the crypt are the words from Napoleon's will: *"Je désire que mes cendres reposent sur les bords de la Seine, au milieu de ce peuple français que j'ai tant aimé."* He had not, of course, thought of the Invalides as his tomb—and it must be admitted that he is not exactly lying by the banks of the Seine—but the Eglise Saint-Louis possesses that atmosphere of *gloire* which the Emperor would have approved.

THIS IS an extremely—some would say excessively—partial view of Paris in some of its aspects. It is not even an attempt to list the most beautiful or my favorite parts of Paris—how could I, with those criteria, omit the Place Vendôme at night, or the rose windows in Notre-Dame, or Lauzun's *hôtel* on the Ile Saint-Louis, or the streets running down from Saint-Germain des Prés to the Quai Malaquais, or the stately interior of the Lucas-Carton restaurant, or the window displays at Fauchon, or the Louvre, or the Rue de Fürstenberg, or the Train Bleu at the Gare de Lyon, or the view from the steps of the Madeleine down the Rue Royale across the Place de la Concorde . . . or . . . or?*

But what of the Parisians themselves? John Russell precisely describes the myth. "Paris would be great, some people say, if it weren't for the Parisians. Parisians—so they say—are abrupt, edgy,

---

* *I have left the Goutte d'Or, the Faubourg Saint-Martin, and the Jardin des Plantes to Professor Richard Cobb's inimitable pen, because no one else could do poetic justice to the unknown quartiers of Paris.*

rapacious, egoistic, and smug." Parisian drivers are the worst in the world, Parisian waiters the most supercilious, Parisian concierges the greediest, Parisian porters the most disobliging. And so the catalogue rolls on. It is not mere foreigners who show their disapproval so vehemently and so repetitively. French men and women in Provence and Languedoc, Normandy and Burgundy, all seem to be consumed with disgust at the behavior of those appalling Parisians. Or is it envy?

It is perfectly true that there is a certain briskness about many Parisians. They are usually in a hurry (but so are New Yorkers, so are Londoners) and sometimes display a slight impatience when faced with stupidity. But they are also as courteous and helpful as any other inhabitant of any other capital city throughout the world. Let Dorothy Menpes deliver a salutary corrective.

> The Parisian is a delightful creature; but he wants approaching. You must know how to soothe and flatter him in order to gain his confidence. You must not mind him thinking that there is no place in the world like Paris. In his opinion Paris is the pivot upon which the whole world revolves, and he will not hesitate to tell you so. He will draw comparisons between his own and other cities; but you must not mind. He will probably look upon you with compassion, because you had the misfortune not to be born in Paris; but praise his city, wax enthusiastic over it, and you will be his friend for life. He will take you by the arm and call you *Mon cher*. As his friendliness increases you will become *Mon vieux*. Be sure to talk to him in French: he dislikes foreign languages. If you meet him thus far you will soon discover what a charming person he is. What will perhaps impress you most will be his light-heartedness, his appreciation of *la joie de vivre*. He knows how to live amiably, to take pleasure in small things. He loves to play with his children: he finds real pleasure in picnicking with them on the grass; or in such small matters as watching the marionettes, superintending the sailing of a toy boat, and floating a captive balloon. Paris is beautiful because the people will have it so. Beauty is to them not a luxury, but a necessity. Perhaps it is this love of beauty and this joyousness that constitute the charm of Paris.

Perhaps, too, the impressionable Dorothy Menpes was observing Paris and the Parisian through spectacles excessively *cou-*

leur de rose. Perhaps even manners and the general *manière de vivre* have deteriorated over the last three-quarters of a century. But it is, nevertheless, high time that someone praised Parisians as well as their city. Some of the glow from the *ville lumière* must surely be allowed to irradiate its inhabitants.

iii

The Moral Climate

ONE OF the best guides to the current state of social change, and above all to any shift in sexual morality, is the free magazine distributed to hotels and listing the activities available to the tourist in any particular week. No doubt any capital city in the world provides a similar service, though there must be gradations in both accuracy and frankness. Some sociology graduate should compose a thesis on one particular section of these magazines, which could be loosely classified as nocturnal pursuits.

Paris has such a magazine, entitled *Allo Paris*. It is a perfectly respectable organ of the press and contains much useful information, lists of theaters and cinemas, restaurants offering both French and foreign cuisines ("*Raspoutine, le restaurant cabaret Russe en vogue des Champs-Elysées, orchestre tzigane, orchestre de balalaikas*," an advertisement with a particularly ferocious sketch of the saintly man, quite disagreeable enough to put you off your blinis), art galleries and museums, shops and beauty salons, tours in and out of Paris—in other words the general paraphernalia designed to part a tourist from his money.

The longest and most detailed section in *Allo Paris* addresses itself to extramural activities. Five pages are headed "*Théâtres Erotiques.*" It should be said immediately and unequivocally that these theaters do not include such well-established institutions as the Folies Bergère, the Lido, the Moulin Rouge, or even the Crazy Horse. They would be considered so unexceptionable in these enlightened times that whole busloads of great-aunts could be entertained there without a blush suffusing the collective cheek. No, these *théâtres érotiques* are something quite different.

Let us inspect some of the display advertisements on those five pages and see whether they give a clue to French sexual taste or, more probably, to what the French consider foreign sexual taste to be. Some are relatively banal. La Fontaine des Amours, situated pleasingly in the Rue des Innocents, for instance, offers nothing more outré than "2 exhibitionist couples and authentical life-shows" (all *sics* will be omitted in the succeeding extracts because they would take up too much space). For 150 francs, you could move on to Le "23" Shocking Show (there is nothing magical about the number 23; that is merely the club's address in the Rue Saint-Denis, not the number of girls involved) and feast your eyes on "the newest, hottest theatre in Paris"—sadly, no air conditioning, even though the show is presumably designed for an American audience—"the most bewitching girls perform with torrid, delirious, shocking, overwhelming realism . . . Exclusive show: a Couple in 'Close-up.' "

The Théâtre Saint-Denis is more teasing, suggesting the alternative pleasures of "*Chinoiseries, Initiation, Jeux Interdits, Sexmania,*" something, one would have thought, for everyone. Not so, however. Let us proceed to the Rue de la Ferronnerie and the Théâtre les Nouveaux Innocents (no one under the age of eighteen admitted, whether innocent or not). The advertisement is something of a masterpiece. It is in both French and English, a comforting thought to those readers beginning to suspect that no self-respecting Frenchman would go within a mile of these establishments. It also has a delightful illustration of a young lady wearing a very short skirt and a great deal of no doubt completely natural blond hair, bending over and apparently attempting to touch her toes; sadly, she seems to have only one arm. She is no doubt limbering up for "*Ici Paris Sex*," billed helpfully as "everything which is *hard* in Paris." In the afternoon, she is evidently not expected to exhaust herself—"an impudent daring hard of an 'up to date' couple and Valerie"—saving her energies for the evening show which seems interminable in its ingenuity: "first public tests of swaping couples; super hit life-shows between women, couples, groups and solo; very wicked strip-teases; projections of triple X films never yet seen; distribution of highly confidential magazines; free drinks at will." And very necessary, too!

It is easy to mock the language of the sex adman, but what is an advertisement for "Love in Paris" doing in a magazine of supposedly general interest? In this case, no holds are barred. Triolism and lesbian shows seem rather *vieux jeu* by now, but there is a great deal more exotic in store: "SM" at 5:45, on Monday, Tuesday, and Wednesday, "*citadelle de la souffrance*" and during the second half of the week "*l'école de maître tyran.*" It is a positive relief to know that Love in Paris does not take place on Sundays. And though it is nice that they welcome Visa and American Express, and that flagellation, *le vice anglais,* is catered for in a voyeuristic way, these cannot be a great consolation to the directors of the Grand Palais and the Centre Georges Pompidou when they leaf through *Allo Paris* to check that the details of their new exhibitions are correct.

However preposterous these examples are, the fact cannot be avoided that France and sex have always been inextricably linked. Visitors from abroad have noted this phenomenon down the centuries. Some have been aghast. Some have pretended horror. Many have thrown caution to the winds and dived into the cesspit. Many have come to France for that precise purpose and have satisfied their curiosity with total abandon.

There has certainly never been any lack of availability. Theodore Zeldin, in his definitive book on France between 1848 and the end of the Second World War, provides some extraordinary statistics. In the 1850s, Paris was thought to have about 34,000 prostitutes, 10,000 more than London, which had double the population. Official brothels, in other words *maisons de tolérance* supervised by the *police des moeurs* (the vice squad), numbered 180 in 1810, at the height of Napoleon's power and when Paris was not exactly overrun by foreign tourists, and had risen to 200 by 1840. By the Franco-Prussian War (1870–71) their number had declined to 145, and in 1892 there were a mere 59.

This diminution should not, however, be taken as an indication of moral upsurge, far from it. The huge increase in unauthorized brothels provided the answer. Between 1871 and 1903, about 155,000 women actually registered as prostitutes, but nearly three-quarters of a million were arrested by the police on suspicion of being prostitutes. In 1900, the *maison de rendezvous* was introduced by the Prefect of the Paris Police. An entrance fee of forty francs was set, and with that sole proviso these new brothels were neither registered nor inspected; the girls did not live there, they merely came there to work. As Zeldin says, "the pleasures of the middle class were thus liberated from state control." It was a peculiarly French situation. The Prefect, in effect, gave his authoritative approval to brothels, provided they were clean, well run, and free of perversions. "Since brothels are considered as public places, any person committing, in an establishment of this kind, in the presence of other persons, an act of immorality constituting a public outrage to modesty, will be prosecuted." The Prefect's war cry was positively evangelical: "No more peep-holes, no more turpitudes." But, as Zeldin points out, this noble endeavor was doomed. "Flexner, the American investigator into European prostitution during the war, was amazed by Paris's specialisation in every kind of perversion, and the way the brothels rivalled each other in inventiveness."

The Prefect's efforts to sanitize illicit sex may provoke a wry smile, but he was only the personification of a generally sensible attitude toward the demands of the flesh. Controls and regulations were introduced every now and then, and there were wholesale closings of brothels in certain cities (interestingly, these included Grenoble, Strasbourg, and Nancy, all on the east side of France and perhaps more influenced by the bracing winds coming up from the Alps), but life went on much as before. Nature abhors a vacuum, a sexual vacuum above all others. If a brothel was forcibly closed, a clandestine establishment would materialize literally overnight. And the soldiers and sailors continued to be catered for. Red-light districts remained in every major port, and semi-official brothels were set up for troops stationed in colonial outposts. It was as late as 1946 that *maisons de tolérance* were outlawed.

High-class establishments could not be dismissed so easily. The reason for their immunity was simple. Far too many politicians and *hommes d'état,* both home-grown and imported, made use of these discreet and luxurious seraglios, half salon, half bordello; a word in the right ear was all that was needed. Gossip about cabinet ministers and church dignitaries, even the occasional President of the Republic, who expired in unfortunate circumstances degenerated into jokes about coitus interruptus and rigor mortis, but there will always be a place in society for the *poule de luxe.* It is a state of affairs prevalent enough in other countries, but the French are less hypocritical than the Anglo-Saxons in their reaction to the fact that our elders and betters are not necessarily in favor of monasticism. Theodore Zeldin remarks on this development after 1918:

> Brothels always existed to cater for every class, but with time some became more like department stores. Between the wars several old firms in Paris were expanded from grubby slums into palatial establishments with armies of girls always available, including Saturday and Sunday, and offering themselves at a low fixed price. These brothels changed hands for large sums. Some owners built up chains of them. More and more girls, however, set themselves up as luxury prostitutes operating more discreetly. It was estimated that whereas in 1789 only 10 or 20 per cent of prostitutes were luxury ones, about a half are today.

Tout passe. Fashions and morality change. Brothels and prostitution flourished for a number of salient reasons. The Church continually emphasized that the sexual act was exclusively for procreation and never for pleasure, and the influence of the Church was very considerable, particularly in the country and in the provincial towns. (It still is, of course. Until recently, contraceptives were absolutely taboo.) There may have been many small-town Emma Bovarys filled with romantic ideas, but their passions went unrequited. Sex education was unknown. Girls were told nothing, boys were left to find out on their own. Thus, girls waited for the marriage bed and, more often than not, a disagreeable experience; boys progressed straight from masturbation to the local brothel. And after marriage, fulminating about his wife's supposed and forgivable frigidity, the married man saw no reason to abandon the nearest available prostitute.

Since the 1960s, there has been a revolution in sexual mores, much frowned on by the Church. Young men and girls live together before marriage, and even if pregnancy occurs, marriage is likely to take its time. Brothels, inevitably, no longer have the same importance. Their educational purpose has vanished, leaving only their function as a refuge or an almost nervous release, when the sexual act is often less crucial than the sympathetic ear. In an age of frankness or permissiveness, call it what you will, the furtive secrecy of the room in an *hôtel particulier* is as out of date, for the young at least, as the similar release of the confessional. Theodore Zeldin, when conducting interviews for his book on the French, encountered a Parisian maid, aged forty, married to a foreman, who frequently went with her husband to pornographic films. " 'I should like to see everything, to know everything about life.' She gets pleasure from hearing people groan when they make love; 'the other day, I heard my mistress doing that in the next room, she was shouting loudly, and I listened and I was pleased, very pleased. I am like her; I need to shout.' She goes with her husband to sit on the terrace of a Pigalle café on Saturday nights, to watch the prostitutes: it is fun watching. For her, sex is to be relished like food; it is nice to look at it as well as to enjoy it." So perhaps, after all, there is un unbroken line in French attitudes to sex, and it is most easily perceived in, of all things, French literature. Laclos's essentially eighteenth-century *Liaisons Dangereuses* is not a million miles from the *Story of O,* nor the Marquis de Sade from *Emmanuelle.* The only aspect that has changed is that sexual freedom is no longer the prerogative of the upper classes.

The French attitude toward homosexuality has also remained remarkably constant. Henri III was assassinated, but the motive was one of religious extremism and not because he had dressed up in women's clothes and surrounded himself with pretty young men. Louis XIV's brother, Monsieur, was blatantly effeminate, even in an age when the most masculine courtier was a fop. But homosexuality, up till the nineteenth century, though widely practiced, only rarely became a source of prurient interest, as during the trials of Gilles de Rais and of the Knights Templar. It was, of course, proscribed by law but was more likely to be thrown into the legal melting pot when other accusations proved too flimsy. In the nineteenth century there were certainly prosecutions and scandals, but remarkably rarely considering the level at which homosexuality was practiced. Male prostitution was described as "an industry of almost unbelievable dimensions."

Homosexuality was denounced by many, but often in a spirit of bewilderment, not merely horror. Larousse trumpeted in the 1860s: "With all its disgusting and ignominious horrors, how can it exist in an advanced civilisation like ours? Unbridled debauchery, blasé sensuality can to a certain extent explain homosexuality but it is difficult in many cases not to admit a veritable mental derangement in the moral faculties. What can one say indeed of one of these men come down from a high position to the lowest degree of depravation, drawing into his home sordid children of the streets before whom he kneels with a passionate submission before begging from them the most infamous pleasures?"

By the end of the century, persecution seems to have evaporated. Proust, Huysmans, and Gide wrote openly about homosexuality, and Robert de Montesquiou made it socially acceptable. Oscar Wilde was generally welcomed as a great writer fallen on evil times, not denounced as a convicted pederast, though the authorities thought otherwise. While he was alive, he was merely cut by British visitors to Paris; after his death, there were problems about his interment. Between the wars, the pace of liberalization quickened. It was the time of Cocteau and the Ballets Russes, of Coward and Cole Porter. Like Isherwood's Berlin, Paris attracted homosexuals from London and New York because there was no need there for sham and pretense. The Princesse de Polignac's salon was always open, actors and painters and musicians of what Wilde termed the Uranian persuasion mingled both intellectually and sexually.

Zeldin underlines the extraordinary freedom:

> In 1937 it was claimed that homosexuality was coming out into the open in all classes, and that there were at least a quarter of a million homosexuals in Paris, with the police keeping files on some 20,000 of them. The clubs, restaurants and baths

they frequented made them into something of a separate world, to which theatrical and literary celebrities gave both notoriety and respectability. They claimed the protection of the Napoleonic Code, one of whose authors, Cambacérès, was said to be a homosexual, but they were still subject to bullying from the police. In the state *lycées*—where it flourished much more than in the church schools—it was of course still vigorously and unsuccessfully repressed. The notion that homosexuality was a symptom of the aberrations in family life was very slow to be accepted.

So it was freedom with danger, but it was a freedom nevertheless, which was shared by female homosexuals. They, too, had sought for many years the comparative tolerance of France. Gertrude Stein and Alice B. Toklas put down strong roots. Radclyffe Hall and Una Troubridge came and went. Romaine Brooks and Natalie Barney presided. The *boîtes de nuit* were full of women in dinner jackets, monocles, and carrying long cigarette holders. What would they think of today's twenty-franc *"show permanent de Lesbiennes,"* from ten in the morning until midnight in the Rue Saint-Denis?

The question must be asked. Have attitudes in France to sex and to the sexes changed radically over the last decade? It is not simply a matter of pornography, or of people taking their clothes off on South of France beaches, or of the decrease in the number of brothels, though all these phenomena no doubt have their relevance. But has the relationship between a man and a woman, between the generality of men and women, altered fundamentally? There is certainly some evidence to support such a claim. The French woman in the nineteenth century was thought of as the most fortunate female in the world. If that was the reality, perhaps there was little competition. No doubt she had a certain matriarchal power; if she was a woman of fashion and married to a rich husband, there were worldly compensations. But was her position any different from that of any other woman in similar circumstances anywhere else in Western civilization? And were these compensations enough? Sexual enjoyment in marriage and the attainment of orgasm were not so very long ago neither discussed nor even imagined, let alone experienced. In a survey carried out in the 1950s, only a small percentage of French women questioned said that the physical side of marriage was enjoyable. Twenty years later, another survey showed that only 13 percent of women actually wanted more sex. In the 1980s, less than half the women interviewed used any form of contraception. Have the old sexual shibboleths really been laid to rest? Undoubtedly not, but their potency has diminished. People are more ready to air and discuss their feelings, something which would have been impossible only a short time ago. Women expect more. Men, perhaps, are unaware of what is expected of them. The attitude of Frenchmen toward their wives or lovers is less prone to change than that of Americans, because the layers of tradition are deeper.

Theodore Zeldin tells an interesting story to illustrate the point. A woman in her early thirties had had an affair with a man some years previously. She had found the relationship immensely satisfying sexually, but broke it off because of his unfaithfulness. Months passed, and then the man reappeared and proposed marriage. A happy ending? Well, not quite. "He has become the best of husbands, loving, thoughtful—and faithful. But for him marriage is incompatible with a rich sexual life. He makes love like a husband. There are no more long sexual games. He caresses me mechanically, always the same way, without any variety. It is a boring habit. And when I express other desires, he exclaims, 'But this is what marriage is.' In short, he said goodbye to excitement when he left his mistress." And the irony is that the wife and the mistress were precisely the same woman. This anecdote says much about the change in the sexual stance of the woman in France, but it also sheds light on the Frenchman's attitude to sex, to marriage and to his own role as provider of both. It is both universal and peculiarly French.

In any analysis of sexual mores at any period of history, the absurdities and contradictions are legion. While total nudity becomes commonplace on any beach, teenagers say they are not in favor of the kind of free love which a hippie commune provides. While the Saint-Denis *théâtres érotiques* exploit the public's apparent fascination with lesbian sex, leaders of liberation groups speak passionately in favor of women's rights. Pornographic and erotic books and magazines proliferate, and less than half the female population use the pill or a diaphragm. Have the French always been more adept, more ingenious lovers? Are they more promiscuous; does the legend of the *cinq à sept*—those two hours set aside for sexual dalliance—prevail? Are the farces of Feydeau an accurate picture of French sexual appetite? The façade is certainly there. Paris and a dirty weekend are still inextricably linked in the minds of vast numbers of Anglo-Saxons. Our forebears licked their lips over the pages of *La Vie Parisienne;* editions of *Ulysses* and *Lady Chatterley's Lover* were readily available in Paris bookshops years before they could be bought in London or New York, let alone Dublin; and literate and literary erotica is still an important part of the French publishing industry. The Lido and the Moulin Rouge continue to exercise their charms. The awful word "naughty" seems almost to have been coined to sum up many people's conception of Paris.

But what lies behind the façade? Are the changes fundamental, gradual, or nonexistent? Is it a question of *plus ça change, plus c'est la même chose?* It is impossible to prove anything, for obvious reasons. But the flicker of sexual heat remains.

iv

A la Carte

BRILLAT-SAVARIN is generally credited with twenty aphorisms, the most famous of which is "Tell me what you eat; I'll tell you what you are." Only a Frenchman could have contemplated a book with the title *The Physiology of Taste* (it was published anonymously in 1826), and only a Frenchman could, in complete seriousness, have adumbrated such a series of dictatorial, pompous, and entirely sensible regulations. For Brillat-Savarin took food very seriously indeed, and his book can quite reasonably be considered the foundation stone of an industry, an art, and a way of life. Nowadays, at least outside France, the great culinary sage is probably best remembered for a particularly delicious creamy and rich cheese named after him, one of those 365 cheeses over which Charles de Gaulle shook his head. (Or has the number now reached 500, since even the French do not know when to call a halt, and continue to invent quite unnecessary cheeses?) But it is his essays on taste and the art of eating which remain his true memorial. The word "art" has already been used twice in this chapter and will be used often again, for in France cooking and, of course, eating have been elevated to an art.

Inspect a few more of Brillat-Savarin's aphorisms. "The discovery of a new dish contributes more to the happiness of mankind than the discovery of a star." An eminently sound opinion. How many people, if they are being honest, really care about stars, black holes, or quasars? How many even care what they are? Surely a new way with sole (or, more likely these days, monkfish, that once deeply unfashionable fish which was rumored to masquerade as lobster in dubious restaurants, but which has now, under its more attractive French name of *lotte*, become quite à la mode) is indeed more important, simply because it gives more pleasure.

"The destiny of nations depends on how they are fed." Here we have echoes of Napoleon's dictum about an army marching on its stomach, and British readers with memories of the Second World War and its whalemeat, snoek, Woolton pie, and other fraudulent conversions will perhaps connect the surrender of Empire and the disintegration of moral standards with what everyone was eating, or not eating, in the 1940s. But even a cynic would allow that Brillat-Savarin had a point, though it is not perfectly acute.

It is, though, perhaps with some of his later aphorisms that Brillat-Savarin displays that particular French view of food which brooks no interference. "A dessert without cheese is a beautiful woman with only one eye." "One becomes a cook; but one is born a *rôtisseur*." (Significantly, there is no English equivalent, the word "roaster" sounding absurd.) "The mistress of the house should always make certain that the coffee is excellent; and the master, that the liqueurs are of the first quality." "To imagine that it is not necessary to change the wine during the meal is a heresy; the tongue becomes saturated; and after the third glass, even the best wine creates nothing more than a dull sensation."

Oddly enough, the origins of haute cuisine rest more in Italy than in France. It was the two Medicis, Catherine and Marie, who introduced such novelties as ice cream and fresh vegetables: spinach, artichokes, savoy cabbage, and broccoli. Even then the Venetian ambassador to Paris could not disguise his general disapproval of the French way of eating. Writing in 1577, he criticized their excesses and their emphasis on meat to the exclusion of bread and fresh fruit. It was not until 1655, when Pierre François de la Varenne published his *Pastissier François,* that a recognizable style of French cuisine began to evolve. His ideas were indeed revolutionary. According to Reay Tannahill in her *Food in History,* he "frowned on spices and on thick meat-and-almond mixtures. He recommended sauces based on meat drippings, combined merely with vinegar, lemon juice (still an expensive luxury in France), or verjuice (the juice of sour grapes, or sometimes of sorrel, green wheat, or crab apples). He provided sixty recipes for the formerly humble egg, treated vegetables as food in their own right, made much use of the globe artichoke, described stuffed mushrooms, and even had a kind word to say for truffles." Here already there are early signs of so-called nouvelle cuisine, and it is appropriate that one of the most celebrated schools of cookery in Paris today should carry la Varenne's name.

The eighteenth century saw a refining of la Varenne's basic views, and only in 1803 did another vital ingredient in the mystique of French excellence in the kitchen emerge with the publication of Grimod de la Reynière's *Almanach des Gourmands.* But the real star in the new firmament was Antonin Carême. This extraordinary man was born five years before the outbreak of the French Revolution and, by his death at the age of forty-nine, had exercised a profound influence on European attitudes to food. He worked for Talleyrand, the Tsar of Russia, the Prince Regent, and Baron Rothschild. He insisted on the very best ingredients and on unlimited funds with which to obtain them. He agreed with la Varenne in his disapproval of overpowering spices and herbs, and on the necessity of extracting the nutritive juices from foods by rational cooking. As a student of architecture, he was also fascinated by the look of the food, by the composition of each dish so that it delighted the eye and not merely the palate. His creations, as recorded in contemporary prints, were indeed beautiful in an extravagant way. One feels that they were meant to be admired rather than eaten.

Carême's pyramids and exotic shapes were architectural in their design. They also very rapidly became cold because they were on display. But he had no doubts about the position of the *maître-chef:* he was "a god on earth." He saw cooking as "the most ancient of the arts and the art which has rendered the most important services to civil life." As Theodore Zeldin says, that was by no means the end of it. "It should be a science too, embodying knowledge of agriculture, chemistry and pharmacy; but to have full scope it had to be treated as a form of showmanship and advertising. . . . Carême argued that once the value of cooking of this kind was appreciated, cooks would be recognised as men of great importance: they should not stay in the kitchen but come out to the dining-room to supervise the eating; they were in fact doctors, with far more influence on their employers' well being than the charlatans who posed as doctors."

Carême was a supremely arrogant man, utterly convinced of his own genius. He had no truck with economies and was often accused of catering only for millionaires. He maintained that his recipes must not be tampered with or simplified. If people could not afford them, they should save up until they could: "Better give two great dinners than four mediocre ones." And the dinners were undoubtedly great. The menu for one given by the Prince Regent in the Royal Pavilion, Brighton, on 15 January 1817, is proof enough. First, four soups, including a rich brown potage containing foie gras, mushrooms, truffles, and Madeira, a vegetable broth, and a fish soup *à la russe;* then four fish dishes—a highly decorated eel, a turbot in a lobster sauce, a matelote of freshwater fish, and trout with tomato and garlic sauce. The remains of the eel and the fish stew were removed, and replaced by what Carême called *grosses pièces* or *pièces de résistance:* a *rond de veau royal,* some chickens with truffles, a braised goose, and a spit-roasted ham with a Madeira sauce.

Surrounding these *pièces de résistance* were thirty-six entrées, which included dishes of salmon, pheasants, rabbit, chicken breasts in breadcrumbs, sweetbreads, a sirloin of beef, partridges, and even a kind of macaroni cheese. So much for the first course. All this was followed by eight set pieces, intended more to impress than to be enjoyed (one was entitled "The Ruins of Antioch"); roast chickens, grouse, cockerels, and wild duck; and thirty-two entremets, which ranged from truffles roasted on coals to oysters, and from pineapple cream to stuffed lettuce. And just in case a momentary pang of hunger might be felt, there were always the *assiettes volantes:* fillets of sole, fillets of wood grouse, potato soufflés, and chocolate soufflés.

The choice and range were overpowering, but the method of approach on the part of the diners was entirely different from that of a modern dinner party or banquet. *Service à la française* and *service à l'anglaise* both implied a free-for-all. After the soups had been removed, everything else was placed on the table simultaneously and the guests were left to forage as best they could. This habit did little for table manners and demanded, ideally, long arms and determination. As late as 1852, Abraham Hayward recalled the discomfiture of a young divinity student asked to dinner by an archbishop and finding a dish of ruffs and reeves, birds much esteemed by gastronomes, placed in front of him. "Out of sheer modesty the clerical tyro confined himself exclusively to the dish before him, and persevered in his indiscriminating attentions to it till one of the resident dignitaries (all of whom were waiting only the proper moment to participate) observed him, and called the attention of the company by a loud exclamation of alarm. But the warning came too late: the ruffs and reeves had vanished to a bird, and with them . . . all the candidate's chances of . . . preferment."

But by then, *service à la russe,* which approximates to the modern method of proceeding course by course, had become common. Carême, too, was dead; his extreme richness compounded of lavish sauces, the most expensive ingredients, and a kind of sculpted magnificence was out of fashion and favor. His successor, Urbain Dubois, often described as *cuisinier de Leurs Majestés Royals de Prusse,* criticized Carême for his extravagance and was a considerable influence on that amateur gourmet and cookery expert Alexandre Dumas. The nineteenth century has many examples of the phenomenal industry of writers (one thinks of Balzac and Scott and Trollope, but the list is a long one) but few could rival Dumas père in his compulsion to put pen to paper. His *Grand Dictionnaire de Cuisine* saw the light of day in 1873, three years after his death. It ran to some 600,000 words, though for some reason it boasted only two illustrations. It is a wild, ebullient stew of advice, prejudice, information (much of it inaccurate), and scholarship. It took Dumas over a hundred pages actually to reach the dictionary entries, offering perhaps a record in the number of preliminary pages; these included a long introduction, Victor Hugo's description of a model kitchen, a protracted letter to Jules Janin, a gastronomic calendar borrowed from Grimod de la Reynière, and, as if he could not bear finally to start his dictionary, another preface.

Here, he sets out his aims. Having reminded his readers that he is the author of four or five hundred books (his vagueness is either charming or disingenuous), he states firmly that he has not written a book of imagination and wit in the style of Brillat-Savarin, nor has he intended a practical book like *La Cuisinière Bourgeoise*. No, his aim is to be read by the sophisticated and used by the practitioners of the art. "What especially tempted me, the indefatigable traveler who had voyaged through Italy and Spain, countries where one eats poorly, and through the Caucasus and Africa, countries where one does not eat at all, was to indicate all the ways of eating better in the former category of countries and of eating somehow or other in the latter category; granted that to achieve this result one would have to be prepared to do one's own hunting and foraging." And Dumas was no counterfeit Tartarin de Tarascon, he was a skilled hunter.

In the dictionary, Dumas dilates on a vast range of subjects, from absinthe (a little joke about the poet Alfred de Musset absinthing himself too often) to the zest of a lemon. We discover that the Lapps are particularly fond of angelica, that it was Poles in the suite of Stanislas Leczinski who introduced the boletus mushroom into France, that really good chocolate should be left overnight in a porcelain coffeepot, that you can educate geese to turn a spit, that lapwings' eggs are popular in Belgium, how to make an Arab omelette, Dumas's views on the plum pudding, "a farinaceous dish without which one cannot have a really good meal in England," a recipe for shark pie, and another for "Welch-Rabbit" (he recommends Gloucester cheese and cayenne pepper).

Because of Dumas's exuberance, it is worth giving one complete entry from the dictionary, in Alan and Jane Davidson's translation. And what better than his dissertation on frogs?

> There are many types of frog which differ in size, colour and habitat. Frogs which live in the sea are monstrous, and are not used as a foodstuff, nor are frogs which live on the land. The only frogs which are good to eat are those which live in

the water. They must be taken from very clear water, and those chosen should be well nourished, fat and fleshy, and should have a green body marked with little black spots. Many doctors in the Middle Ages were opposed to the idea of people eating this meat, which nevertheless is white and delicate and contains gelatinous matter which is more liquid and less nourishing than that of other meats. Bernard Palissy, in his *Traité des Pierres* of 1580, expressed himself thus: "And in my time, I have observed that there are very few men who have wanted to eat either tortoises or frogs."

And yet in the sixteenth century frogs were served at the best tables, and Champier complained of the taste for these, which he found odd. And it is just about a century ago that a man named Simon, from Auvergne, made a considerable fortune on frogs which were sent to him from his part of the country, which he fattened and then sold to the best houses in Paris, where this food was very much in style.

In Italy and Germany, there is a very large consumption of these batracians, and the markets are covered with them. The English are horrified by them, and no doubt for this reason they used to make, about sixty years ago, caricatures showing the French eating frogs.

They should read this passage from the history of the island of Santo Domingo, written by an Englishman named Atwood: "There are," said he, "in Martinique many toads which are eaten. The English and the French prefer them to chickens. They are fricasseed and used in soup."

Frogs are prepared in several different ways, mostly in soups which are very health-giving and which are even used by some women to maintain the freshness of the complexion.

Dumas's eccentric dictionary had very little influence on French cuisine, even though it contained many good recipes and much sound advice. It was Escoffier who was acknowledged as the next great innovator. He realized that the age of the *pièce de résistance* had passed, that people no longer had the time or the patience (let alone the money) to lavish on sumptuous dinners stretching on course after course. He discarded Carême's basic *sauce espagnole,* a complicated and exceedingly rich reduction of game, meat, and fowl, and aimed at simpler, more attainable dishes. He maintained that he created his best recipes for ladies, who had more delicate appetites. His famous (in Elizabeth David's view, notorious) recipe for *pêche Melba* was originally nothing more outré than peaches and vanilla ice cream served up between the wings of a swan carved in ice, as a tribute to Dame Nelly Melba's appearance in *Lohengrin;* the *purée de framboises* was added later.

Escoffier was an entirely novel kind of chef. He was not attached to a great house, to a French duke, or to a Rothschild. Instead, he reigned in the grand hotels which were springing up all over Europe. He advised César Ritz, and he worked for many years at the Savoy and Carlton hotels in London. Entertaining was moving progressively away from the private to the public. Restaurants proliferated, and by the beginning of the twentieth century it was considered quite *comme il faut* for women to eat out. Not that Paris had ever lacked restaurants. Although there were less than fifty at the outbreak of the French Revolution, by 1820 there were nearly three thousand. Restaurateurs made fortunes, retired to country estates, entered politics, were looked up to in a way unthinkable in London or New York. Gastronomic guides, the forerunners of Michelin and its imitators, began to appear. Cookery books became increasingly popular, some advocating a return to Carême's standards, others aimed at the bourgeois family. Audot's *La Cuisinière de la Campagne et de la Ville* went through forty-one printings between 1833 and 1900, and *Le Cuisinier Gascon* and *La Cuisinière Bourgeoise* were continuing best-sellers. The Academy of Cooking was founded in 1883.

The beginning of the twentieth century was dominated by Curnonsky (his real name was Maurice Sailland), a man of vast girth and innumerable ideas. He advised the firm of Michelin, and put his views into practice by driving around France in search of restaurants and specialties. His findings were published in 1933 in *Le Trésor Gastronomique de France,* a distillation of no less than twenty-eight books written by Curnonsky over the previous three decades. To Curnonsky, more probably than to any other man, goes the credit for revealing to the Parisian that there were other restaurants out there in the provinces, particularly in Lyons and in Provence; cars and food were an enticing combination. He established the four types of French cooking: *haute cuisine, cuisine bourgeoise, cuisine régionale,* and *cuisine improvisée.* He seems to have spent the major part of his life in persuading his readers to raise their standards and their expectations, to be more adventurous, to avoid the old-fashioned restaurants which concentrated more on quantity than on quality. No wonder he was elected

Prince of Gastronomes in 1927. (And can one imagine such a title being conferred on anyone in America or England, where an interest in food was considered at best eccentric and at worst a sign of moral degeneracy?) Fired by this honor, Curnonsky proceeded to found the Académie des Gastronomes, a club limited to a membership of forty. Among those elected were the Prime Minister, the playwright Maeterlinck, the secretary-general of the Paris Opéra, and—no doubt a wise precaution—a doctor from the Institut Pasteur.

Curnonsky did not die until 1956, demonstrating at the age of ninety-four that obesity and a lifetime of what one might call investigative eating are not always a killing combination. Perhaps the thin wartime years put a mild curb on his appetite; certainly, there were considerable privations for the gourmet forced to live on his memories. Something of this feeling is given by Gertrude Stein when she returned to her beloved France:

> I came back to Paris after the long sad years of the Occupation. I will tell all about that, and I wandered around the streets the way I do and there in a window were a lot of etchings and there so pleasantly was one by Dufy, it was an etching of kitchen utensils, in an inspired circle and at the bottom was a lovely roasted chicken, God bless him, wouldn't he just have a lovely etching by him in the window of a shop and lots of kitchen utensils, the factories could not make them, but he had, and the roast chicken, how often during those dark days was I homesick for the quays of Paris and a roast chicken.

The *faux-naïf* style perfectly, movingly, catches the moment; one can almost smell the good butter, perhaps a pinch of thyme, perhaps a piece of lemon rind, above all the fat, succulent farm-reared chicken.

Things improved rapidly. Soon after the war, Alan Houghton Brodrick wrote a marvelously evocative book, *Cross-Channel,* in which he describes a visit to Montpazier, that perfect fortress town on the way to Cahors. It is an unabashedly lyrical passage by a man in love with France, and it should be quoted in full.

> Come to Montpazier any time of the year and you will eat well. The thick stone walls are cool in summer and warm in winter, for the wind can whip cruelly about this upland.

Then, the low lights of the wood fires seem good after the brilliant grey-green hill-frosts of early winter.

The food is prepared over a fire in a vast open hearth. The cauldrons, pots and saucepans hang black upon the ratchet. Wood-pigeon and partridge turn on the spits. The dry vine-shoots crisply crackle as the place fills with their blue aromatic smoke and tingling odour.

This is, indeed, no place to get fussy dishes à la Cambacérès [Jean-Jacques, Duc de Cambacérès was Napoleon I's Arch-Chancellor and a great gourmet, though Carême considered him penny-pinching; any dish called after him will contain foie gras], but go when the game is on and you will eat food for outdoor men and it must be, one likes to think, very like the rustic cooking of the Romans.

The kitchen is in the hall and you can eat with an eye upon the spits and sizzling pots. That's the way to enjoy a meal, but, luckily, I have run across nowhere in France that peculiarly Iberian combination that used not to be rare in Spain: stable, kitchen, bedroom and dining-room all in one—that's very Low Latin indeed.

Maybe the main dish will be lièvre à la royale. There are plenty of thyme and herbs and long runs hereabouts. The hare are tasty.

Now hare done in Royal Style is a real piece into which go not only your hare and a belly of pork but white wine and meat juice, pears and prunes, garlic, herbs, onions, chestnuts, mushrooms, truffles, red wine and ham. It's not a city dish. Like all game (and even that glutinous horror, rabbit), the Royal Style is better experienced in the country.

But before the main dish you will get a fine, thick soup in a deep bowl. Real soup and nothing like the plash of skilly offered us here. None of your timid soup-plates for this juice of the civet. If you like a substantial opening to your meal you will, if wise, pour into the soup a quarter of a litre of red wine and drink the whole from the bowl without any new-fangled soup-spoons. This fashion of lapping it up is called by the men of the South-West faire Chabrol. No one seems to know why. Perhaps some member of that ancient southern family was a noted gourmet.

Then, depending upon the days, there may be some fish, but we're a good way inland for anything but trout or crayfish. Ecrevisses can be good enough served in a heaped scarlet buisson, a veritable Burning Bush of Crayfish. But such things are, as they say, *pour amuser la gueule*—to amuse the muzzle. We get right down to the *civet à la royale*. . . .

And then come along a brace of *palombes* or wild doves and then the other half of the hare, well grilled. . . .

The sweet-meats, the *entremets*, will be, as always, the weakest part of this rustic meal. Better eat some home-made jam and fresh cream and then tackle the cheeses of the country. Roquefort is their glory and although there are not here such magnificent soft cheeses as Brie and Camembert (at their best), still, the strong and subtle cheeses of the South are worthy of all respect.

Down here, after all, one is near the Lot and it may well be that the wine is the fruity, purple southern vintage of Cahors, city of Popes and prelates and prunes and memories of pomp. Nearly all the *Côteaux du Lot* are interesting and well sustain the Périgord cooking that ranks with those of Burgundy, Provence, Bresse and Béarn as the best in the French provinces.

This extract neatly sums up two of Curnonsky's categories, *cuisine bourgeoise* and *cuisine régionale*. What of *haute cuisine?* It would be easy enough to describe any number of Paris restaurants, but let us instead take a provincial town. There is, of course, no such thing as a typical French provincial town, simply because each part of France provides its own particular reversion to type. Blois may seem the perfect example, only to be superseded by Amiens (an ugly choice, in spite of the cathedral), or by Dijon, or by Montpellier the minute the traveler has established himself* in any of these towns and absorbed in his mind's eye the requisite number of indications of typicality. If he chances to arrive by train, the railway station will provide an immediate sign. Then he will look for a suitable quantity of avenues and boulevards devoted to the memory of those political giants of the past, many of whom have faded into that state of semi-oblivion which is reserved for statesmen and warriors. There ought to be Gambetta, probably Jean Jaurès, Clemenceau, and de Gaulle sine qua non; though only rarely will one of those prime ministers of the post–Second World War period—coming and going as if in a bewilderingly complex formation dance—materialize. Perhaps only the largest cities are massive enough to accommodate them all.

* *I hope my female readers will forgive this example of male chauvinism. For "he," please read "I."*

After the street names (and no doubt the complementary statues), will come the cafés and restaurants, to one of which we will shortly proceed; the plane trees, the church spires, the cheaper variety of chain stores, the little parks (more statues), the relics of the past, the views (perhaps even a panorama), possibly a river for the essential fishing and *canotage*. But this is little more than an identikit picture, the bare essentials without the wrinkles, without indeed the character. Let us, therefore, be specific. Let us choose Vienne.

Vienne lies on the Rhône, not far from Lyons, not far from Grenoble, in the *département* of Isère. It is a rich culinary area, but no one would accuse Vienne itself of being important, or dynamic, or influential. In certain respects, it is not even particularly beautiful, and yet it possesses to an extraordinary degree the charm of provincialism. In Roman times, it was important, and there are temples and excavations and even a lapidary museum to prove it. There is also a curious obelisk, something like Cleopatra's Needle, which the French will insist on calling a *pyramide* (an immediate clue to the student of the red Michelin, though the connection will escape those who read only the green Michelin, which prefers monuments to restaurants). Vienne possesses, too, a fine church of near-cathedral proportions, narrow streets often cobbled, an astonishing proliferation of *pâtisseries* and *boulangeries,* a street leading down from the railway station to the river which boasts a string of cafés much frequented by ample ladies with a taste for *bombe surprise* and *café liégeois,* as well as a one-rosette restaurant which serves an admirable *salade gourmande* with crayfish and foie gras, municipal gardens whose chef d'oeuvre is a harp totally confected from flowers, a fine view from the opposite bank of the Rhône, and more than enough plane trees.

In short, Vienne is as typical of French provincialism as . . . well, as a hundred other French towns. And yet there is a crucial difference, one which Curnonsky would have spotted immediately. Even today, if you mention Vienne to any Parisian who aspires to some culture and discrimination, he may not even be aware of those temples and churches, let alone the floral harp. "Ah," he will say, with a distinct quickening of interest, "I remember a particularly superb . . ." And he will fall happily into those nostalgic culinary quicksands which open up before any Frenchman with taste, appetite, and a suspect liver.

What that one word "Vienne" has done to him is quite as effective as Pavlov's bell, and it stimulates the salivary glands in much the same way. What he is about to reminisce over is, *bien sûr*, a restaurant, but not just any restaurant. For Vienne's real reputation is based solely on what is, strictly speaking, the Pyramide (named after that preposterous obelisk) but what is generally called, simply, "Chez Point." Fernand Point founded the restaurant—the admiring citizens of Vienne even called a street after him—and his widow presided until her death in 1986. The Pyramide is one of those few rare restaurants outside Paris on which the exacting inspectors of the Michelin guide bestow the maximum number of rosettes; in 1985, only fourteen restaurants outside Paris were awarded three rosettes. Recently there have been disagreeable mutterings about a falling-off of standards, suggestions that the Pyramide retains its rosettes because the Michelin inspectors did not wish to hurt the ancient and tender feelings of Madame Point. My only visit to this gastronomic mecca occurred some years ago, and then there could be no doubt that the inspectors were right.

For, just as Vienne can be allowed to represent provincial France, so, too, can Chez Point stand for the great restaurants. Of course, all such establishments, particularly if they have been in existence over a number of decades, acquire a certain patina of style, of reputation, of history indeed. The Pyramide, according to one American gourmet, "combines lavish plenty with the irreproachable *grande cuisine* of the early 1900s and with what is even more a talisman of aristocracy: faultless, smiling, unhurried, considerate service by everyone in the establishment." Now he was writing a quarter of a century ago, long before the revolution in French cooking brought about by Paul Bocuse and his confrères (of which more anon), and when the *méthode* Point did not encompass such fripperies as menus or even wine lists. Then, apparently, Monsieur Point's cellars contained *"eleven* of the best years of Romanée-Conti and *ten* of the most celebrated Château d'Yquems." The italicization was justified, as no doubt was the somewhat overheated summing up: "the loftiest tabernacle of gastronomy in France today."

Such laurels are hard to wear; they have a tendency to slip comically over one ear. Perhaps the service is a little less faultless, a little less smiling, though my allergy to oysters was not frowned upon and a dish of perfect foie gras was offered instead. Perhaps the duck could have been a touch more tender. But the décor is pleasing, the flowers are nicely arranged, the *plateau de fromages* is extraordinary, the sorbet offered to cleanse the palate satisfactorily timed, the entremets dazzling, and the wine list positively fabulous (prices to match). It is no doubt much as it always has been; the sense of tradition and permanence is comforting.

The ritual, though, has altered. The late Aga Khan's favorite table, reputed to have been hydraulically supported owing to his huge girth, is still on view, and it was indeed the behavior at that particular table which caused more astonishment than did the food. Ensconced were two transatlantic gentlemen, one vast, one small, bearing a startling resemblance to Sydney Greenstreet and Peter Lorre in *The Maltese Falcon* or *Casablanca*. At least the vast one was ensconced; his diminutive friend popped up and down taking flashlight photographs, of the restaurant, the food, the waiters, the other diners, and Mr. Greenstreet himself.

It was all mildly disturbing, but no worse than that. The effect on the staff at the Pyramide, though, was more pronounced. In particular, the antique sommelier seemed barely able to retain his encrusted equanimity when the immense American ordered a bottle of pre-phylloxera* Latour. General consternation! (Though, I observed mildly to myself, If you find such an item on the *carte des vins* and can afford to pay for it, why not?) Would it actually be drinkable? Great ceremonial ensued. The bringing and displaying of the sacred bottle, the uncorking, the sniffing, the sipping after a very short interval—all mercifully appeared to be well. The restaurant relaxed. The meal proceeded. I noticed that our neighbors, Messrs. Lorre and Greenstreet, had opted for the *menu prestige,* richer in quality and containing two additional courses. But then the host had a large area to fill.

Some hours later—such meals should not be hurried—movements signifying departure emanated from the left. A request was made for a wine list (bound in red leather) and for the famous bottle of Latour, now empty. Lorre took a final photograph. Greenstreet rose . . . and knocked the bottle to the floor. Shards of glass, gasps of horror, but also a curious restrained mirth. The

---

* *The phylloxera aphid, an import from America, destroyed French wines during a twenty-year period after the Franco-Prussian War and cost France 12 billion francs.*

odd couple left in a bad temper. The atmosphere eased once more. Drinks all around. The comedy was over.

So much for haute cuisine, its pleasures and its dangers. But what of the ordinary Frenchman and his family, who have never heard of the Pyramide, and who may never have been to Paris? Theodore Zeldin refers to a study of 547 bourgeois households between 1873 and 1953. According to this study, eating came high on comparatively few lists of priorities; on average, between 21.5 and 25 percent of a family's income was spent on food, but these average figures concealed a wide range between 14 and 34 percent. By 1980, the average middle-class family was spending more on food than on anything else. The London *Daily Mail* picked the LeBras family, husband and wife both in their mid-thirties, with two children aged three and nine respectively. André LeBras worked as a senior telephone technician, his wife Françoise taught English at the local school in Rennes. Their joint annual income was just under £15,000 (about $30,000); they had daily help, and they took a month's holiday every year. Their weekly expenditure on food—and one must assume that this embraced wine and spirits—amounted to about five hundred francs per week. Françoise LeBras did not have a deep-freeze, preferring to buy fish and meat as needed, concentrating these purchases at a big covered shopping area. A large supermarket was the main source of supply, but Françoise also patronized a certain number of speciality shops, especially for meat, cheese, and *pâtisserie*.

There has inevitably been a leveling both up and down in culinary habits. Well-organized hypermarkets abound throughout France, but they are still supported by the speciality shops, which appear to flourish. Because so many more women work, the importance of the delicatessen and the supermarket open late has greatly increased. There is even a trend toward restaurants selling their products, either direct or via an attached shop, at prices considerably lower than would be paid in the restaurant itself with all its overheads. Fast food is another development. Without doubt, standards have coalesced: The rich less likely to have a full-time resident cook and therefore prepared to cut corners; the middle and working classes eager to enjoy what is advertised on television, even though it may have far less nutritional value than the old *cuisine bourgeoise* dishes. The standard everyday French restaurant menu, concentrating on a *salade panachée*, either trout (probably frozen) or a steak with *frites,* a poverty-stricken selection of cheeses and an exhausted-looking apple tart brought in, begins to look almost attractive when one is faced with the alternative of the universal hamburger.

At the other end of the scale, there are those two twin developments, *cuisine minceur* and *nouvelle cuisine,* both essentially contradictions in terms. *Cuisine minceur* was always rather absurd, ostensibly an effort to cater for a new, young generation obsessed with exercise and waistlines, often in reality an excuse to palm off the minimum quantity of food at the maximum price. The menu may well say *salade d'écrevisses.* The result could be, as I have experienced, a plate of assorted greenery, topped with four microscopic crustaceans, a few slices of the inevitable kiwi fruit, and, to set it off, a daffodil placed rakishly at one corner. The price for one mouthful—unless one is particularly devoted to fashionable types of lettuce, in which case three mouthfuls—could be seventy-five francs. The consolation of having devoured so few calories may not be sufficient.

Nouvelle cuisine, too, is not especially new. A number of gifted chefs have returned to basics, borrowed from Escoffier and Boulestin, even Brillat-Savarin, and created a style where, again, small can be beautiful. Very beautiful indeed sometimes, as it is often difficult to judge whether a dish put before you is to be eaten or admired. These gastronomic paintings, however, owe nothing to Carême, but are derived rather from Oriental sources, primarily Japanese. Roses sculpted from tomatoes, sauces bearing Japanese hieroglyphics, the exact angle at which each slice in a *magret de canard* is set to its neighbor, the way a *coulis de fraises* enhances its companion *bavarois,* the design of a spun-sugar basket, the positioning of the three minute purées of vegetables—all these considerations are held to be as important as the main ingredients. Everything must be underdone, so that all meat and game is pink, all vegetables have barely passed the stage of rawness. At its best—an increasingly rare occurrence—*nouvelle cuisine* is subtle and delicious. At its derivative worst, it is merely pretentious and shockingly expensive.

Does it matter? The answer is yes and no, yes because fashion always matters, no because there is always a new fashion just over the horizon. And without doubt it is the basic French cuisine and the basic French attitude to food which really matter. Elizabeth

David, who is worth a hundred Escoffiers or Troisgroses, shook her head sadly, in an article written in 1980, over the standards in far too many French restaurants. She found three reasons for this collapse: the quality of the actual raw materials, the skill of the cooks, and the customers' critical faculties. She observed too many traveling salesmen, once sure indicators of a good reasonably priced establishment, swallowing inferior dishes without a murmur of complaint. She experienced a simple *oeuf sur le plat* stuck hard to the serving dish because it had been so roughly cooked. She found bad manners and impatience and discourtesy.

But she also found many reminders of the good old days, at both ends of the market, a restaurant in Lyons as good as it had ever been, a young couple taking endless pains in an out-of-the-way hotel, shops providing everything one ever dreamed of for the perfect picnic. No doubt Madame Poulard's famous omelettes at the Tête d'Or in Mont-Saint-Michel still follow the basic recipe as laid down by her in a letter to Robert Viel back in 1932: "I break some good eggs in a bowl, I beat them well, I put a good piece of butter in the pan, I throw the eggs into it, and I shake it constantly. I am happy, monsieur, if this recipe pleases you." The *pré-salé* lamb is still unbeatable, Alan Houghton Brodrick's *lièvre à la royale* smells just as rich and enticing, the *beurre blanc* sauce is as frothy and delicate as ever.

And one can indeed always fall back on a picnic. Elizabeth David wrote this piece on the market at Montpellier twenty-five years ago, but the facts have not changed.

Here in England we find little in our local delicatessen shop—the only approximation we have to the *charcutier* who sells many ready-prepared foods besides pork-butchers' products—but mass-produced sausages, pork pies and fish cakes off a conveyor belt, piled slices of pale pink and blood-red flannel which pass respectively for cooked ham and tongue, bottles of pickled onions and jars of red cabbage in vinegar, possibly a potato salad dressed with synthetic mayonnaise and, with luck, some herrings in brine. In any French town of any size at all we find perhaps three or four rival *charcutiers* displaying trays of shining olives, black and green, large and small, pickled gherkins, capers, home-made mayonnaise, grated carrot salad, shredded celeriac in *rémoulade* sauce, several sorts of tomato salad, sweet-sour onions, *champignons à la grecque,* ox or pig's muzzle finely sliced and dressed with a vinaigrette sauce and fresh parsley, a salad of mussels, another of *cervelas* sausage; several kinds of pork pâté; sausages for grilling, sausages for boiling, sausages for hors-d'oeuvre, flat sausages called *crépinettes* for baking or frying, salt pork to enrich stews and soups and vegetable dishes, pigs' trotters ready cooked and breadcrumbed, so that all you need to do is to take them home and grill them; cooked ham, raw ham, a galantine of tongue, cold pork and veal roasts, boned stuffed ducks and chickens . . .

Delicatessens in New York and London have improved out of all recognition since 1960, but outside the major cities matters go on much as ever. The appalling ersatz *taramasalata*, a vicious pink mess with no relationship to smoked cod's roe, and a few other pseudo-ethnic monstrosities have joined the potato salad and the Bismarck herrings, but that is the only bow in the direction of change for the better. In France, too, matters go on much as ever, though the range has become even wider and includes more *plats composés*.

Theodore Zeldin sums up the state of the art (or of the science, as Escoffier would have it): "The prosperous English worker kept his tastes even when moved into the middle class; but the French peasant who ended up as a bourgeois sought to become, at least in his eating habits, a minor seigneur. The French have also put much more effort into propaganda about their food and they exported a very large number of cooks, whereas the English sent abroad more colonists, missionaries and administrators."

Perhaps that is why the English gained (and lost) a great empire, whereas the French were content to export a cuisine. It is a cynical observation which will not stand scrutiny, but is it not remarkable how many former French colonies have retained so many aspects of French life, but above all the care for and appreciation of food? Brillat-Savarin would be both pleased and totally unsurprised.

V

Wine and Water

I N 1852, GUSTAVE FLAUBERT made the following pronouncement: "All of us Normans have a little cider in our veins; it's a bitter, fermented drink, which sometimes bursts the bung." In Normandy, cider is important, as is calvados. The intoxicating still cider or lighter *cidre bouché,* a kind of apple champagne, should be cherished. And calvados—whether the cheaper kind which can make amazing improvements to a pork chop with apples or to a chicken or pheasant cooked *à la vallée d'Auge,* or the venerable bottles which are suspiciously vague about age—is far more dependable than most cognac, and much better for you.

However, it must be sadly admitted that the great majority of French men and women (disregarding those unfortunates who live beyond the French borders) do not connect cider with France. Instead, reasonably, they think of wine. A slight but important correction is necessary. They think of wine and they also think of water.

Advertising and presentation have become extremely important in recent years, and the purveyors of wine and water are equally insistent in their passionate desire to introduce to the general public their spendid products. Now such vulgarities are, of course, frowned on by the owners of vineyards in Bordeaux, in Burgundy, in Alsace, and even in the Loire. (Loire wines, once relatively neglected, were discovered, their cheapness was applauded, and they were turned into a cult; now they threaten to become as expensive as white burgundy, which had virtually priced itself off the market.) But the so-called lesser wine-producing areas of France have woken up to the fact that their wines are perfectly drinkable, often rather more than that, and that they compete highly favorably with all those expensive, lordly clarets and sauternes. But they must advertise in order to compete properly, and very impressive the copy is. Here is, retained in French to keep the full flavor of the richly lilting persuasion, the message conveyed on the label of a very nice *rosé frisant*. It will be noticed that the layout resembles that of a poem by Apollinaire, who was not, incidentally, responsible for Apollinaris water.

> *Ce vin légèrement pétillant*
> *Provient d'un terroir exceptionnel*
> *Douze hectares de Grèzes glaciaires*
> *Du type médoc ou bourguignon*
> *Accrochés sur un contrefort du Larzac*
> *Au pur soleil du Languedoc*
>
> *Culture organique et désherbage manuel*
> *Production faible 35 hectos/hectares*
>
> *Rosé de pressurage en grains ronds*
> *Cabernet sauvignon 1/3*
> *Syrah 1/3 Viognier 1/3*

Très lente vinification à 16°
Sauvant tous les arômes de fruit
Et gardant le gaz naturel fermentaire
D'où le goût pétillant—frisant

Vin de soleil à boire frais
Vin de bonheur à boire heureux

La vendange 1984 a produit
*6,250 bouteilles**

It would be impolite to mock. After all, there is a great deal of information contained there. We know the types of grapes used, the soil on which the vines were grown, where the vineyards are, even how large they are, roughly how the wine is produced, the year of the vintage, and the number of bottles produced. Who could ask for anything more? But there are two phrases—*"au pur soleil du Languedoc"* and *"vin de bonheur à boire heureux"*— which transcend mere information and fill one with a wild desire to uncork the bottle without further delay and to drink.

That is the soft sell. The alternative is much more aggressive: "Sir, will you remain skeptical if I try to convince you that a Côtes de Provence Appellation Contrôlée can nourish any ambitions higher than those provided by mere holiday wines, fit only to wash down a *salade niçoise?* . . . Of course not! And yet . . ." And then the splendid phrases begin to roll: *"une grande tradition," "le redoutable Carignan," "à l'honneur des cépages nobles."* "And finally . . ." And we know that all the proprietor's efforts have not been unavailing. Gault and Millau, once the Castor and Pollux of French gastronomy, now separated, say so. Odette Kahn of the *Revue de Vin de France* says so. Even the Institut Technique du Vin de Bordeaux concurs. *"Bon bouquet," "très belle*

---

* *A free translation, lacking the poetry of the original, would go something like this: "This lightly sparkling wine originates from an exceptional soil, twelve hectares of Grèzes dating from the pleistocene period, of the médoc or burgundy type, clinging to a spur of the Larzac range in the pure sun of Languedoc. Organic culture and removal of grass by hand, scant production 35 hectos/hectares. Rosé wine from the pressing of plump grapes, a third Cabernet sauvignon, a third Syrah, a third Viognier, very slow vinification at 16 degrees thus preserving all the aromas of the fruit and retaining the natural fermenting gas which produces the sparkling taste—the fizz. Wine of sunshine which should be drunk cool. Wine of happiness which should be drunk in a happy state. The harvest of 1984 produced 6,250 bottles."*

couleur," "du caractère," "personnalité remarquable," even *"très nerveux":* the plaudits ring, and, one is happy to report, quite right, too.

But all these highly pressurized words are certainly not limited to the wine industry. Water has its own account executives and copywriters. Take this as an example. "Volvic springs from a huge natural filter of porous rock in the volcanic mountains of Auvergne in Central France. Its source goes down to a depth of several hundred feet through massive layers of volcanic pozzolana, basalte and andesite, all of which have special filtering qualities. It is protected by 43 square kilometers of forest and sandy moorlands. It is the unique structure of the soil through which Volvic percolates that gives it its light and balanced nature." *Indubitablement.* But they have not finished. The label has a pretty map showing in which direction Clermont-Ferrand lies, the altitude of the Puy de Dôme (1,465 meters, for those who are interested), and the various layers of subsoil. We are told how much water passes through our bodies every year (220 gallons), and the importance of choosing the right water is emphasized. There is a chemical chart to show what Volvic is made of. The French Ministry of Health gives its imprimatur. And we are assured that the water is suitable for a low sodium diet. The bar-code and price seem an afterthought after so many words.

None of this is wasted. The war of the waters is ferocious and never-ending. Water has always been drunk with meals in France, sometimes to dilute a strong red wine but generally in order to help the long-suffering liver to combat too much rich or heavy food. But water has become big business. Perrier, the market leader for so long, has ceased to relish the slightly snide designation of "designer water" and prepares to do battle with Badoit, the water most approved by the French wine trade because its bubbles are smaller and it is a little saltier. Perrier maintains that the gas in its water has been evolving over 140 million years, but its days of supremacy seem to be fading. Still waters like Evian and Volvic are coming up in the world. And it seems a world gone mad. As an article in the *Financial Times* put it in August 1985, "It is one of the great oddities of our day that this staff of life should have been turned into a successful market commodity—that all of our historic feelings about the importance of our drinking water should end up incarnated in a green bottle modelled on an exercise club. This has come about in ten years. We seem hardly to have realised what has happened—that, in a way, good fresh water has again become a luxury, one of the significant privileges of wealth." How surprised Evelyn Waugh would be. In his diary, he recorded dining at the Ritz: "I imprudently drank two bottles of Vichy water before starting, fell ill, and had to leave the table to be sick." Nowadays we drink bottled water in order to ward off illness, or drunkenness. And the French manufacturers, who provide such a superb service, cannot be blamed if they make a great deal of money in the process out of what is, or should be in the best of all possible worlds, absolutely free.

Why do we drink it? It is not bacteriologically cleaner than water from the tap. But it is supposed to be better for us than wine, and at least it is harmless. But is that reason enough? David Sexton in the *Financial Times* provides the necessary reasons. Bottled water may, of course, *taste* better than tap water, though interestingly enough a blind tasting in New York came out in favor of tap water. And then should we also make our ice cubes out of bottled water? The second reason is bizarre. It is "entirely to do with the fact that it is bottled and pricy and, ironically, offers a service purely by virtue of that. It can be seen to cost something, and so satisfy honour when money must be spent or hospitality received. This makes it socially useful: a positive choice that is not alcohol." In other words, the purchase of mineral water is linked with financial snobbery, demonstrating that the host has enough money to lavish on something which could just as easily come free, or more or less free, from the tap.

The third reason is equally odd. Sexton defines it as "political." "It represents the exercise of private choice in preference to public provision, which can seriously be seen as a good in itself."

So Badoit and Perrier, Vichy and Evian, let alone San Pellegrino and all the British bottled waters, will continue to fizz and bubble or just lie flatly in the glass. The profits of the companies will continue to soar as long as the health fad continues to soar. Health is an industry, and water is part of the industry. It is all very strange.

But at least bottled water is unlikely to harm you. Such a claim can no longer be made with any confidence about wine. Recently there has been the Austrian scandal which revealed that antifreeze had been added to certain wines, and the more serious

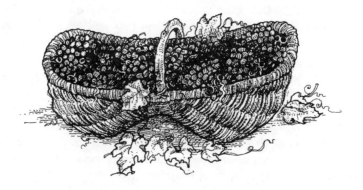

scandal in Italy, where wines from Piedmont and the Veneto were found to be so toxic that they could—and did—kill. But the greatest scandal of all broke in Bordeaux in 1974. It came to be dubbed "Winegate" and reveals rather too much about the greed of certain shippers. It is a cautionary tale with more than a touch of farce.

The basic problem was, as it so often is, supply and demand. During the late 1960s and the early 1970s, the wines of Bordeaux became big business. Because first the American and subsequently the Japanese markets expanded with unexpected vigor, prices went up, values at auction soared, and prices rocketed. Suddenly the whole basis of the claret industry changed from a gentlemanly affair to one of competition and the need to survive. Nicholas Faith, in his riveting book *The Winemasters,* quotes Peter Sichel: "Up to 1971 in an average year a grower of Bordeaux Rouge even if he sold his entire crop probably had to borrow money to finance the production for the following year. Today he can finance 1973 by selling only half his crop. In St. Emilion or the Médoc he only needs to sell twenty-five per cent of his crop. Perhaps a first growth could cover its costs by asking shippers to pay for their samples."

There was no problem about cash—so long as supplies lasted. The production of French wines is governed by a series of strict regulations. The ownership of a *cru,* in effect the actual vineyard and its reputation combined, is jealously guarded, and it was considered an event of unprecedented novelty when Mouton-Rothschild was deemed worthy to join the big four *premiers crus:* Lafite, Margaux, Latour, and Haut-Brion. But it was not these grand labels which were affected by the boom, simply because nothing could be done about quantity without quality succumbing. In the lower reaches, however, there were no such limitations. The AOC wines (*appellations d'origine contrôlée*) were suddenly challenged by the inferior VDQS wines (*vins délimités de qualité supérieure*). One *négociant* laid on a tasting, actually in Bordeaux, of wines from the Rhône and Beaujolais. The highly respectable firm of Calvet began selling VDQS wines from formerly unremarked areas of France, and marketed a new brand called "Vieux Calvet"; it had no *appellation* (basically, a label guaranteeing that a particular wine comes from a particular area) and was not guaranteed to have been more than one year in bottle.

Such a situation cried out for someone prepared to bend the rules. Pierre Bert was the man. Nicholas Faith describes him:

> He had learnt to love wine but to despise the rules which surrounded its sale—an attitude highly convenient for anyone whose livelihood depended on turning the law's restrictions to his own ends. For Pierre Bert possessed all the attributes required in someone destined to expose the essential hypocrisy of French wine laws—and the tricks of those who had to comply with them. He was and remains a compulsive exhibitionist, a trait which has invariably led him to expose many of his schemes to discovery by the police, the Ministry of Agriculture's Fraud Squad, or the tax authorities (he displayed this compulsion early in life: he was clever enough to be considered for the prix d'honneur at the Jesuit School he attended, but ruined his chances by being caught singing the "Internationale" in the street just before the prize-giving).

Bert was an engaging rogue. He devised an admirable way of making money, based on the switching of certificates. "If Bert could buy ordinary red wine and AOC white, and then switch the certificates so that he was selling ordinary white but AOC red, he would lose only 10 percent by demoting the white wine while gaining 300 percent by promoting the red." Because the demand for red wine far exceeded that for white, he had hit upon a superbly simple and profitable scheme.

Bert went into business with the Cruse brothers, Lionel and Yvan, and everything proceeded satisfactorily. Of course, it could not last. There was a tip-off and the gentlemen from Bordeaux's tax office duly descended on Bert's office and warehouse. Both Bert and the Cruse family took evasive action, and the tax officials had to apply to Paris for authority to search the Cruse cellers. President Pompidou was dying, and two men were preparing to fight to succeed him. Jacques Chaban-Delmas happened to be a friend of the Cruses; his rival, Valéry Giscard d'Estaing, was not. Giscard d'Estaing was Minister of Finance. It was he who provided the authorization to the tax officials. The case went ahead, the prosecution now turning its attention to the allegation that the Cruses had used chemicals to doctor the inferior wine which they intended to pass off as AOC.

The trial was set to open on 28 October 1974. The prosecution based its case on a voluminous document prepared by the Fraud Squad. Summarized, it went as follows: "The different examples quoted below—which may not be the only ones—demonstrate that the firm of Cruse respected neither the idea of *appellation* (because c c wines [*consommation courante,* in other words non-vintage] were given the names of AOC wines, or that a lot of one *appellation* was divided into shipments bearing the names of different *appellations,* or that they mixed AOC with c c wines) nor did they respect the idea of a *cru* because the same wine could bear different châteaux names, nor the idea of a particular vintage, because dates were allocated to wines which lacked them when they arrived in the cellars."

It was a technical case likely to be understood by the expert witnesses but not, as it transpired, by the judges, who became totally muddled. There was only one microphone, and without it most of the evidence was inaudible. Pierre Bert, unlike the Cruses, enjoyed every minute. He was outspoken in his opening statement: "I am guilty but it was not I who invented fraud. There are thousands as guilty as I . . . I didn't do anything very original. Out of 1.5 million hectolitres entitled to be labelled Bordeaux, there are 700,000 to 800,000 that are magnificent. The rest are little Bordeauxs, modest wines, that cannot be offered to a foreign clientele. . . . There are two markets for Bordeaux. For the second market there must be a mixture. The mixers are the vineyard owners and the sellers. And they sometimes make a good mixture."

What Bert was saying, of course, was that he was one of very many, that in fact most *négociants* and owners of vineyards did much the same, and that these mixtures, though not suitable for the discerning export market, were quite good enough for the French. His views were not views designed to make him popular, but that was not a consideration which gave him a moment's worry. He preferred to instruct the judges. One of them asked him, with some surprise, whether he had actually mixed white and red wine. Bert opined that the addition of white wine did no harm, particularly when the red possessed too much tannin. The judge: "Yes, but it's not legal." Bert: "No, but it's good."

The Cruse brothers stood up well under cross-examination. Lucien Castaing, one of Bert's customers, made a good general point about the state of the wine trade: "In 1972, we witnessed incredible follies. Because a number of Anglo-Saxon countries had monetary problems they became obsessed with Claret, which suddenly resembled gold bars; I even had rubber companies and cigarette manufacturers asking me to take their money." But the evidence of Barnabé, the driver who had transported the wine and supervised the switching of certificates, was conclusive. The Cruses evidently knew what was happening. The game was up.

Defense lawyers muttered about prejudice and interference from Paris, always a good card to play in a provincial courtroom. One of them remarked perfectly reasonably that the "body," in other words the wine accused of being adulterated, had not been produced in court, nor indeed subjected to a blind tasting. But it was all to little avail. The prosecution asked for nothing more than a suspended sentence in the case of the Cruse brothers. The three judges departed to consider their verdict, which was delivered on 18 December. Out of the clutch of defendants, ten were acquitted. The Cruse brothers and six others were given suspended sentences. Only Bert was sentenced to a term of imprisonment.

The real results of the case were infinitely more far-reaching. The Cruses' uncle had already committed suicide. Lionel and Yvan, and Pierre Bert, now had to find approximately 3.5 million pounds (or 7 million dollars) to pay the taxmen. The reputations of the Cruses and a number of other people were damaged beyond repair. The workings of the Bordeaux trade had been laid open to the fascinated gaze of the rest of France and to merchants and shippers around the world. Half-truths and dissimulation had tumbled out from a trade which had been considered, foolishly, beyond reproach in its honesty and reliability. Bordeaux would never be quite the same again.

It is almost a relief to add that Pierre Bert wrote a best-selling autobiography while he was in prison. He called it, almost inevitably, *In Vino Veritas*. Nicholas Faith pays him a tribute: "He is the brightest and most engaging of souls, small and perky, witty and literate, able to clothe his cynicism and his misdeeds in a style entirely suitable for an age which cherishes anti-heroes of the requisite quality and panache."

Edmund Penning-Rowsell wrote in November 1976: "To return this autumn to Bordeaux, battered by nearly three years of crisis, is rather like revisiting a friend's family that has been sadly afflicted by an accident, to a degree unknown to the visitor. Who, one asks cautiously, have died, how many are alive and well, and how are the convalescents? In Bordeaux one quickly discovers, not only that the family is very large, but that their circumstances differ widely and that there are some serious family disagreements." Since then, the Bordeaux trade has reorganized itself, relaxing in some ways, tightening in others. The considerable amount of competition from other wine-growing areas of France can only be beneficial. After all, what most people want is drinkable wine, uncontaminated by chemicals, at a fair price, with the occasional bottle of fine, and therefore expensive, wine for special occasions. If one can afford more of the latter category, so much the better.

There will probably be other scandals. There are disturbing rumors of the "rationalization" of the champagne market. There are stories of vast underground vats devoted to quantity rather than quality. It is, sadly, all the fault of the British who drink huge quantities of champagne and need to be constantly supplied at a knock-down price. Like mineral water, champagne demonstrates affluence and consideration for one's guests, even when the latter might well prefer a Vouvray *pétillant* or a Blanquette de Limoux. And the current craze for pink champagne will, no doubt, cause further expansion and profitability in the French wine trade. What the dealers in Bordeaux and Burgundy, in Epernay and Rheims, must long for is a real Watergate. Then they might have it all their way. And so would the Water Board.

vi

Le Vert Galant

THE FRENCH have never felt great affection for their rulers. Reverence was due to Louis IX, but he was a saint. Louis XIV created around him an aura of royalty never surpassed, but he was a distant figurehead to most of his subjects; he swore never to return to Paris after suffering the privations and dangers of the Fronde,* and he kept his promise. A few kings had

---

* *The civil war (1648–53), fought during Louis XIV's minority between the Court—led by Anne of Austria, the Queen Regent, and her chief adviser, Cardinal Mazarin—and the French Parliament. The word* fronde *comes from a presumably violent children's game played in the streets of Paris.*

complimentary nicknames bestowed upon them—Robert II, the Pious; Jean II, the Good; Charles V, the Wise; Charles VI, the Well-Loved—but these seem merely to counterbalance the derogatory sobriquets—the Fat, the Quarrelsome—given to their predecessors or successors.

One exception, however, has always been allowed. Henri IV was greatly admired in his day, and his reputation has not suffered with the passing of the centuries. And one can easily see why. He is, of course, credited with two famous statements, neither well authenticated but both credible. The more celebrated of these dicta was that Paris was well worth a Mass. A few misguided people may have considered this outrageously cynical and opportunistic; most Frenchmen thought it statesmanlike and pragmatic. The second pronouncement—that he wanted every family throughout the country to be able to afford a chicken in the pot for lunch every Sunday of the year—was manifest proof of his generosity, love of his subjects, but above all a sensible attitude to good bourgeois cooking.

In many ways, England's Charles II is a kind of mirror-image to Henri IV. Both men suffered from the miseries caused by religious intolerance and strife; both were voracious in their sexual appetites; both were sensible, accommodating rulers; and both were blessed with a love of the good things of life, above all with a strong sense of humor. One cannot possibly imagine inviting Charles I of England or *le Roi Soleil* to dinner (nor, perhaps, Abraham Lincoln), but both Charles II and Henri IV—like John F. Kennedy—would have been delightful guests.

Henri of Navarre was born in the castle of Pau, in Béarn, down in the southwest of France, on 13 December 1553. His mother was Jeanne d'Albret, daughter of the King of Navarre; his father Antoine de Bourbon, Duc de Vendôme, older brother of the Prince de Condé. His maternal grandmother, Marguerite, had been François I's sister. At his birth, no one would have given good odds on his ever ascending the French throne. The Valois dynasty ruled securely. Henri II still had six years of life, and he had three sons (François II, Charles IX, and Henri III) ready to succeed. Navarre seemed a very long way from Paris, and from the Cathedral of Rheims, where French monarchs were traditionally crowned.

It seems to have been Henri's maternal grandfather, the King of Navarre, who was the greatest influence during his early years. He was evidently a straightforward man who stood no nonsense. When his daughter was about to give birth, he advised her to sing a song, "in order that you may bring me a child who will neither weep nor make wry faces." The minute the boy was safely delivered, his grandfather rubbed a piece of garlic on his lips and gave him some wine, symbols of manliness. Very soon he was taken away from Pau and the influence of his father, and established at Courraze, near the Valley of Lourdes, very much under his grandfather's aegis. He was brought up simply and strictly. There were no French fripperies, and he was encouraged to run wild. He developed an extremely strong constitution.

There is an interesting description of him as a teenager given by a Bordeaux magistrate and later quoted by the Duc de Nevers:

> He behaves towards everyone with such a relaxed air that people crowd round him, and his every action is so noble that one can see he is a prince. His conversation is that of a straightforward man; it is always to the point, and if it turns on court matters, one discovers that he is well-informed, and he never speaks out of line. I shall always hate the new religion for having claimed so worthy a man.
>
> He insinuates himself into all hearts with incredible skill. If men honour and esteem him, women do so no less. They do not find his flaming beard unattractive. His face is well-made, the nose neither too big nor too small; he has gentle eyes, a ruddy complexion and soft skin; his vivacity is so extraordinary that he is certain to succeed with the ladies.
>
> He likes gaming, and good living. When he is short of money he finds means to acquire it, means quite new and as useful for others as for himself. For he sends to those of either sex whom he believes to be his friends a promise in his own hand bearing his own signature, and begs that they will send him back the note or the money. You can imagine that there are not many houses which refuse him. It is held to be a great honour to have one of this prince's notes, and they are received with pleasure, for there are two astrologers here who say that either their art is a fake or that this prince will one day be one of the greatest kings in Europe.

The magistrate was shrewd about Henri's effect on the ladies, and the astrologers were unusually accurate.

The reference to the new religion must be explained, since

the bitter fight between Catholic and Protestant dominated the
age. The Valois kings vacillated. Henri II's widow, Catherine de
Medici, and François, Duc de Guise led the Catholic faction;
Louis, Prince de Condé and the redoubtable Admiral Coligny inspired the Huguenots. In 1563, the Duc de Guise was murdered by
a Protestant. In 1569, the Prince de Condé was assassinated by a
Catholic. There were appalling outrages, as when 150 Catholics
were thrown into a well in Nîmes in 1567. Then, on 24 August
1572, came the worst horror. During what would always be known
as the massacre of St. Bartholomew, over two thousand Huguenots—men, women, and children—were slaughtered in Paris.

Six days earlier, Henri had married his cousin Marguerite de
Valois, sister of Charles IX. It was a loveless match. Marguerite
had to be nudged into agreement by her brother, and Henri
showed a complete lack of interest in the proceedings. The Papal dispensation, demanding that Henri become a Catholic and
impose the Catholic faith on his kingdom of Navarre, did not arrive in time. Within the week, none of this seemed to matter.
Charles, spurred on by his mother, Catherine de Medici, had given
the word for the massacre of the Huguenots to commence. His pu-
sillanimous nature had cracked, and the latent sadism in his character rose to the surface. "Kill them all, so that not one will be left
to reproach me afterwards. Let them all be killed! Let them all be
killed!"

Only his cousins, Navarre and Condé, were spared, mainly because Catherine wanted them as a counterbalance to the overween-
ing ambitions of the Guises. While Catholic Europe rejoiced at the
news of the massacre—Philip of Spain was supposed to have laughed
for the first time in his life—the Huguenot princes reviewed their
futures. Henri was incarcerated in the Louvre and then at Vin-
cennes, only to be released on the death of Charles IX in 1574. The
new king, Henri III, the third of Henri II's three sons, was effeminate and capricious. The Venetian ambassador gave a sharp portrait:

> He has a noble enough bearing, a gracious presence, and the
> most beautiful hands of all men and women in France. His
> manners are serious although from affability he abandons a
> modicum of solemnity and the grave demeanour natural to
> him. He is full of contradictions; his habits, his manner of
> dressing, his love of personal adornment all tend to make him

seem delicate. In addition to his lavish costumes, decorated with gold, jewels and pearls, he wears the most luxurious shirts and hats, and he wears a double gold and amber circlet round his neck which gives off a subtle aroma. But what to my mind detracts from his seriousness most, is to have had his ears pierced like women. He is not content to wear a pair of ear-rings, but needs must wear two on each ear, with hanging pendants enriched with semi-precious stones and small pearls.

Henri of Navarre, robust, plain-dressing, soldierly, must have offered a striking contradiction to all this foppery and self-indulgence. Though he was ostensibly freed, his movements were under constant surveillance. He was not permitted to practice his religion, he was forced to dissemble his real feelings, he was in constant danger of assassination. He wrote to an old friend. "It is the strangest Court you ever saw. We are always ready to cut each other's throats. We all carry our poiniards and all wear mail shirts and frequently a breastplate under our tunics. . . . You would never believe how strong I am in this court of friends. I affront everybody and only wait the opportunity for a fight. For they say they will kill me, and I wish to strike first."

In February 1576, he escaped with a few companions, including the poet Agrippa d'Aubigné while supposedly on a hunting expedition. They rode from Senlis to Châteauneuf in one day, and finally reached safety at Alençon. He swore that he would never return to Paris.

During the next thirteen years, Henri of Navarre showed himself to be a courageous and often brilliant commander in the field. He was quite unmoved by the Bull of Excommunication issued against him by Pope Sixtus V in 1585. The Pope referred to Navarre and Condé uncompromisingly as "two children of wrath, a bastard and detestable generation of the House of Bourbon," and Henri fired off a strong rejoinder: "He says and sustains that Sixtus V, calling himself Pope, has, saving his Holiness, falsely and maliciously lied, and that he himself is heretic . . . he, the King of Navarre, holds him and declares him to be Antichrist and heretic, and in that quality declares against him a perpetual and irreconcilable war."

But Henri's real passion was poured into a series of letters to his mistress, Diane d'Andouins, widow of the Comte de Gramont, and known as "la belle Corisande." Even in moments of exhaustion or despair, he found the energy to write to Diane: "Love me, my all. Your favour is the consolation of my soul in the midst of afflictions; do not refuse me this support. Good night, my life." Henri was credited with having fifty-six mistresses during his life, and as a consequence a huge number of bastard children, to whom he was devoted. But until his meeting with Gabrielle d'Estrées in 1590, Diane de Gramont was the chief recipient of his love letters. Often they were somewhat hypocritical—"believe my fidelity to be pure and unspotted; it never had its like"—but always they were fervent and almost incandescent in their sexual heat.

The Wars of Religion continued to tear France apart. Henri, Duc de Guise, was killed at Blois two days before Christmas 1588, and the instigator of his murder, Henri III, was murdered the following August. Before he died, he bequeathed his crown to his cousin of Navarre. The last of the Valoises passed away on 2 August 1589. Nearly five more years of war were needed before Henri of Navarre could be crowned King at Chartres on 27 February 1594, and even then he was denied the traditional coronation at Rheims because the Archbishop of Rheims was in the hands of the Guises. The great battle of Ivry fought against the Catholic League and a sizable Spanish contingent under Count Egmont was won in March 1590, but Paris resolutely refused to surrender. Finally, on 25 July 1593, Henri decided to abjure and to embrace the Catholic faith. He was following out what he had once told his friend Duplessis-Mornay: "Perhaps the difference between the two religions only appears to be so great by reason of the animosity of those that preach them. By exercising my authority I shall some day try to arrange everything." Paris fell the following March. It had been worth a Mass. Henri was forty years old and had sixteen more years on the throne.

Henri IV maintained that he prayed to God every day for three things: "First that He would be pleased to pardon my enemies; second to grant me victory over my passions, and especially sensuality; and third, that I may make a right use of the authority He has given me and never abuse it." God listened to his prayers on the first and third counts. Henri was extraordinarily magnanimous to his former opponents. When the Duc de Mercoeur, who had held Brittany for the League for ten years, finally gave in, Henri promptly betrothed Mercoeur's daughter to his own illegitimate son, whom he created Duc de Vendôme; and he once referred to himself as "a shepherd King, who will not shed the blood of his sheep, but seek to bring them together with kindness." His use of his authority was assisted and strengthened by the constantly wise advice proffered by one of the greatest statesmen France has ever produced, Maximilien de Béthune, Baron de Rosny and subsequently Duc de Sully. Together, they set about pacifying France, restoring the country's finances and agriculture, which had been devastated by the Wars of Religion, and laying the foundations for the Edict of Nantes, which established the respective rights of the Catholic and Protestant religions, and which was finally ratified in February 1599. Well could Henri declare, when the Treaty of Vervins was signed in June 1598, thus ending the war with Spain: "I have just achieved by a stroke of my pen more exploits than would have been possible in a long war with the best swords in my kingdom." Both Henri and Sully realized that the time of the sword was over and that France desired one thing above all others: peace.

All this time, Henri's other great comforter, Gabrielle d'Estrées, had been maintaining her deep hold on the King's affections. Gabrielle was one of a family of six girls and one boy, who were dubbed the Seven Deadly Sins. It was an immoral age, and her virtue was no more devalued than that of any other court lady. Her amorous career, however, was singular. She had been virtually—if that is the mot juste—sold by her mother to Henri III, who may not have known what to do with her, and then to a financier called Zamet. She then progressed via the Cardinal de Guise to the Duc de Longueville, and then to the Duc de Bellegarde. Her connections were certainly impeccable. In the notorious double portrait of her and her sister, the Marquise de Villars, she stands uncompromisingly nude, though concealed from the waist down, a pearl earring hanging from her left ear, and with her right nipple being pinched by her sister. She gazes steadily at the painter, cool, unembarrassed, self-assured.

Henri was deeply smitten. He wrote: "To spend the month of April apart from one's mistress is not to live. . . . No woman is like you, and no man equals me in knowing how to love. My passion remains the same as when I first began to love you, my desire to see you again is more violent than it was then. In short, I cherish, love and honour you miraculously. . . . I write to you, *mes chères amours,* from the feet of your portrait, which I worship only because it was done for you, not that it resembles you. I can be no competent judge of it, for I have painted you all perfection to my soul, my heart and my eyes."

Eager to sever the sterile relationship with his wife, Marguerite, Henri resolved to marry Gabrielle, whom he had created Duchesse de Beaufort. It was not to be. Gabrielle ate something which violently disagreed with her at a dinner given by her old friend Zamet, and on Easter Saturday 1599 she died. Henri was desolated. He wrote to his sister from Fontainebleau: "The root of my love is destroyed; it will not sprout again." He exaggerated, of course, but he probably never felt quite the same intense passion for another woman, though he would eventually be trapped between the demands of his second wife, Marie de Medici, and two mistresses, Henriette d'Entragues and Jacqueline de Bueil. He did not care for Marie, and wrote complainingly to Sully: "I receive neither society, amusement, nor content from my wife; her conversation is unpleasing, her temper harsh, she never accommodates herself to my humour, nor shares in any of my cares; when I enter her apartment, and offer to approach her in tenderness, or begin to talk familiarly with her, she receives me with so cold and forbidding an air that I quit her in disgust, and am obliged to seek consolation elsewhere." It is a classic case of the misunderstood husband.

Not that Henri was blind to his own faults; one of his most endearing qualities was the ability to see himself plain, though he disarmed his critics easily enough. Sully quotes him analyzing himself:

> Some blame me for being too fond of buildings and great works; others for liking hunting, dogs, and birds; one says that I have a passion for cards, dice, and other kinds of gaming; another condemns me for my attachment to women, to the pleasures of the table, to assemblies, plays, balls, running at the ring, and other amusements of that kind; where, say they, I appear as gay and lively with my grey beard, and am as proud of having gained the goal, and received a ring from some fair lady, as I could have been in my youth, or as the vainest young fellow of the court. I do not deny but there is some truth in all this; but if I am guilty of no excesses in these pleasures, my conduct deserves more praise than blame; and, indeed, some little indulgences I ought to have in amusements which bring no inconvenience upon my people, in considera-

tion of the labours I have endured from my infancy to fifty years old.

Henri was aging prematurely. His life had been a turbulent one, and he had devoted extraordinary energy to matters of state-craft. The Edict of Nantes was safely ratified, and he had thrown himself into an ambitious plan to unite the kingdoms and princi-palities of Europe in a loose alliance against the threatening power of Austria, in which each entity would remain independent unless called on for assistance by another. His robust constitution stood him in good stead. Exhausted he might often be, but he still cut a fine figure. Bishop Péréfixe described him in the last years of his life:

> Henri was of medium height, active and agile, hardened by work and cares. His body was well-shaped, his temperament strong and robust; and he had stupendous health, despite the fact that, by the time he was fifty, he had had several attacks of gout which passed off quickly and left him unscathed. He had a deep forehead, lively and commanding eyes, a long nose and a ruddy colour—in all a noble and calm face, which never-theless betrayed the warrior. His hair was thick and brown, he wore a large beard but kept his hair short. He started to go grey at the age of thirty-five.

He celebrated his fifty-sixth birthday in December 1609. The European political scene looked no calmer, and Marie was insist-ing on a coronation ceremony which would emphasize her posi-tion. Henri was in a state of nervous tension. He was eager to join his army at Châlons-sur-Marne, but felt that he must wait in Paris for the coronation, scheduled for 13 May. He burst out in the Duc de Sully's presence: "I shall die in this city; they [Catholic extrem-ists] will murder me here; I see plainly that they have made my death their only hope. Oh, this cursed coronation! It will be the cause of my death." The coronation ceremony passed off well, but he could not sleep that night. The following morning, he heard Mass at the church of the Feuillants, and walked in the gardens of the Tuileries with François de Bassompierre and the Duc de Guise. He was still in an uncertain mood.

That afternoon he ordered his coach to be made ready, as he intended to drive to the Arsenal to see Sully. Pierre de l'Estoile left a record of what happened:

His coach was held up because a pig and a handcart were blocking the way and he had to stop at the corner of the rue de la Ferronnerie. . . . He was there killed and assassinated by a wicked and desperate good-for-nothing named François de Ravaillac. . . . Ravaillac threw himself upon him in a rage with a knife in his hand and gave him two thrusts in the breast, of which the second penetrated to the heart, cutting an artery, which stifled the King's breath and life so that he could not even speak. . . . They turned the coach back towards the Louvre, from which the King, swimming in blood, was only removed dead.

The autopsy showed that he should have lived another twenty years.

The Duc de Sully wrote a considered memorial, elegiac but balanced:

With regard to the qualities of his heart and mind, I shall tell the reader nothing new, by saying that he was candid, sincere, grateful, compassionate, generous, wise, penetrating; in a word, endowed with all those great and amiable qualities which in these memoirs he [Sully] has so often had occasion of admiring in him.

He loved all his subjects as a father, and the whole state as the head of a family. . . . It was his desire, he said, that glory might influence his last years, and make them at once useful to the world and acceptable to God: his was a mind in which the ideas of what is great, uncommon, and beautiful, seemed to rise of themselves: hence it was that he looked upon adversity as a mere transitory evil, and prosperity as his natural state.

I should destroy all I have now said of this great prince if, after praising him for an infinite number of qualities well worthy to be praised, I did not acknowledge that they were balanced by faults, and those, indeed, very great. I have not concealed, or even palliated, his passion for women; his excess in gaming, his gentleness often carried to weakness . . . but I have likewise observed that his enemies have greatly exaggerated all these errors. If he was, as they say, a slave to women, yet they never regulated his choice of ministers, decided the destinies of his servants, or influenced the deliberations of his council. As much may be said in extenuation of all his other faults. And to sum up all, in a word, what he has done is sufficient to show that the good and the bad in his character had no proportion to each other; and that since honour and fame have always had power enough to tear him from pleasure, we ought to acknowledge these to have been his great and real passions.

There is a fitting memorial to Henri IV in the equestrian statue on Paris's Pont Neuf; the bridge itself was constructed during his reign. Henri adored Paris, no doubt because it was denied him for so many years, and he oversaw the great building works on the Ile de la Cité and in the Place des Vosges. When the Pont Neuf was still incomplete, he jumped from pier to pier the width of the Seine. The Hôtel de Ville was completed, and the Louvre came alive during his rule; sadly, his plans for improving the palace were never carried out, though his wax effigy continued to lie in state there for eleven days after his death, being treated with the same deference which would have been granted to the living monarch.

His statue was painted by Dufy in 1926. Horse and rider look very green indeed, as if the artist wished to convey the spirit of *le Vert Galant*. His memory is equally green. He loved Paris and France, and they returned the compliment.

vii

Châteaux

IN HIS most famous lyric, Joachim du Bellay wrote longingly of his birthplace. He had been born in the château at Liré, between Nantes and Angers on the river Loire. *"Heureux qui, comme Ulysse, a fait un beau voyage,"* the poem starts. Diplomat and courtier, du Bellay imagines himself as Ulysses or one of the Argonauts, having completed a dangerous but triumphant journey, returning home. He yearns for the sight of smoke rising above the small country village, for the unostentatious house better by far than any grand Roman palace, for *"la douceur angevine,"* the sweet fragrance of Anjou, above all for *"mon Loire gaulois."* Sadly, du Bellay almost never returned; the château fell into ruin. But the Loire continued to flow, through some of the most beautiful country and past some of the most exquisite palaces and castles in the whole of France.

It is very difficult not to share du Bellay's nostalgia, his yearning for what later French writers would have termed *"la princesse lointaine,"* that chimeric perfection constantly vanishing into the mist; the *fête étrange* in Alain-Fournier's magical novel *Le Grand Meaulnes* should, like Perrault's *Belle au Bois Dormant,* have been set in the château of Ussé, as prototypical a fairy-tale castle as Segovia is the perfect castle in Spain. If one stands in the forest of Chambord as the autumn leaves are turning red and gold, or looks at the delicate arches of Chenonceaux, or remembers Ronsard spinning his love lyrics in the small château of Talcy, it is very difficult to imagine being anywhere else.

My first sight of the Valley of the Loire—my first real sight of France—was in 1957 at Blois. An unsophisticated, rather prissy, wholly English schoolboy, I had arrived in order to polish my spoken French before Cambridge. A lady with the resonant name of Sallier du Pin and no doubt in straitened circumstances kept a kind of finishing school high up looking down toward the river. Her husband was dead—a distinguished army officer, one surmised, though one never asked—and the rather grand house must have been difficult to keep up in anything approaching a prewar style. There was a garden and a tennis court, so essential in France; there was a cook and a maid and perhaps even a gardener. Madame possessed a car, which could accommodate a remarkably large number of passengers. She had two nephews, one rather supercilious, who mocked what he saw as English seriousness, the second more outré, who would vanish on most hot afternoons to fish and swim with his friend, a future playwright of considerable notoriety.

And then there were the girls. It was not at all like Terence Rattigan's farce *French Without Tears;* there was no romance, let alone sex. The 1950s were an innocent age, and girls who had just escaped from their encircling English boarding schools were still feeling their way. When I was staying in that old house in Blois, they had not yet found it; nor, indubitably, had I. So, though there were occasional visitations by other girls, intent on playing tennis (I was very bad at tennis), the ultimate in temptations seemed to be jugs of orangeade and plates of that mock gingerbread, *pain d'épice* (certainly my equivalent to Proust's madeleine). But that, of course, was not why I was there; more's the pity perhaps.

Instead, there was very gentle tuition in the morning, *précis* and *dictées* and little essays, and discussion of the plays of Corneille and Jules Romains (a curious combination, the latter seeming infinitely preferable then and now), and some local history. The sun shone interminably outside the window, the motes of dust danced in the air, the words of Villon or Verlaine hung heavy. But none of this mattered. For it was the afternoons which were important. Then it was the moment to cram into the car and drive off to yet another extraordinary, extraordinarily beautiful château: Chaumont, Cheverny, Chambord, Chenonceaux, all the best ones seemed to start with "Ch." Looking back, there were certain curious omissions in Madame's chosen itinerary. Ménars was not included, perhaps because there would have been too many prurient questions about the precise relationship between Madame de Pompadour and Louis XV. Nor was Villandry, partly, I suspect, because gardens were considered less educative than buildings, partly because the entrance fee was considered outrageously high. Azay-le-Rideau, one of the most perfect of all the smaller châteaux, was always too far. Valençay and Sully-sur-Loire were no doubt included because of their historical connections, the first with that great cynic and reprobate Talleyrand (can Madame really have approved of him?), and the second with Henri IV's wholly admirable adviser and friend the Duc de Sully.

But there were riches enough: the bloodstained history of Blois and Amboise; François I's salamander and the peacocks in the gardens at Chenonceaux; the double staircase at Chambord and the convoluted hunting horns at Cheverny; Leonardo da Vinci's house at Le Clos-Lucé; first hearing those sad, lilting lines of Ronsard's echoing out over the towers of Blois during a son et lumière:

> *Quand vous serez bien vieille, au soir, à la chandelle,*
> *Assise auprès du feu, dévidant et filant,*
> *Direz, lisant mes vers en vous émerveillant:*
> *Ronsard me célébrait, du temps que j'étais belle!*
> *. . . n'attendez à demain;*
> *Cueillez dès aujourd'hui les roses de la vie.**

* *When you are very old, and sit in the candlelight at evening spinning by the fire, you will say, as you murmur my verses, a wonder in your eyes,*

The Valley of the Loire seemed full of those *"roses de la vie,"* whether they grew neatly in formal gardens surrounded by aromatic box hedges, or whether they had been allowed to run riot by the walls of the dovecotes and *gentilhommières** which lay scattered about the countryside. It is a soft landscape, divided by the slowly moving Loire, but crisscrossed by innumerable streams and rivulets, with dappled cows grazing contentedly along the water meadows. In the forest around Chambord and Cheverny it is darker and more rugged, hunting countryside concealing the wild boar and deer which are still pursued by the extravagantly clad huntsmen who ride out from Cheverny; but there are always clearings, oases of sparkling light, placed surely with intent for a *déjeuner sur l'herbe*. And the river is never far away, the sound of water always around the next bend in the road. Above all, though, there are the châteaux: some, like Loches and Langeais, rather intimidating, castle keeps and dungeons and small dark rooms smelling of blood and fear; some, like Chenonceaux, simply magnificent; some, like Montgeoffroy or Cheverny, pretty and domestic and charming, with the smell of cooking entwined with the smoke from an autumnal bonfire; some like Chambord, like a bright medieval miniature from the *Très Riches Heures*. The splendor falls on castle walls.

Henry James published a little book in 1884, called modestly and appropriately *A Little Tour in France*. In it he records his impressions of the French countryside as he journeyed in leisurely fashion from Tours across to Nantes, down to Bordeaux and the South, and then up the valley of the Rhône to Beaune and Dijon. Characteristically, as his biographer Leon Edel points out, James observed the women he encountered with an analytical eye; uncharacteristically, he wrote succinctly and with a sharpness in description not often present in his novels. He does not, as Edel says, "gulp down the sights, the castles, the old houses, but caters always to his aesthetic nature. We envy him this particular endowment." In my little tour of the châteaux of the Loire, I will superimpose on Henry James's impressions, so vivid and so apt still today, my own, some imbued with the *pain d'épice* of that summer of 1957, some *arrosés* by the sparkling Vouvray of more recent years.

"Ronsard sang of me in the days when I was fair!" . . . *do not wait for tomorrow; pick today the roses of life.*

* *Something akin to a manor house.*

BLOIS LIES mainly on the north bank of the Loire. "It is a very sympathetic little town," thought Henry James. "It presents a bright, clean face to the sun, and has that aspect of cheerful leisure which belongs to all white towns that reflect themselves in shining waters." But, as he soon discovered, Blois is deceptive: "The interior is of a proper brownness, as befits a signally historic city." Without its great castle, it must be admitted, Blois would be no more impressive than a hundred French provincial towns. It has elevation, with its layers of terraces connected by steep flights of steps; it has, like the older parts of Tours, a Balzacian character; and it has the river. But it is the château which dominates. James was impressed, though he noted with mixed feelings the extraordinary amount of restoration. "The Château de Blois is one of the most beautiful and elaborate of all the old royal residences of this part of France. . . . As you cross its threshold, you step straight into the brilliant movement of the French Renaissance."

One of the finest parts of the château does indeed belong to the high Renaissance, but Blois is very far from being a perfectly designed palace, all of a piece. The Tour de Foix, at one corner, was built in the thirteenth century, as was the Salle des Etats; Charles d'Orléans's gallery stems from the middle of the fifteenth century, predating the Saint-Calais chapel and Louis XII's wing;

with the magnificent François I wing, with its external staircase, we do indeed reach the Renaissance; but still to come there is the wing built by Gaston d'Orléans in the seventeenth century. La Fontaine approved of what an unkind student of architecture might term a mess: "These three parts are, thank God, without any symmetry, having neither connection nor conformity one with another. That which was built by François I, seen from without, pleased me the best; there is a great number of little galleries, little windows, little balconies and little ornaments, without regularity and without order; that makes up something great, which is pleasing enough." Whether he would have extended his approval to the final rectangle, after the restorations carried out during the nineteenth and twentieth centuries, is another matter.

Henry James was in two minds. "The long façade, consisting only of balconied windows deeply recessed, erects itself on the summit of a considerable hill, which gives a fine, plunging movement to its foundations. The deep niches of the windows are all aglow with colour. They have been repainted with red and blue, relieved with gold figures; and each of them looks more like the royal box at a theatre than like the aperture of a palace dark with memories." Lightness and grace he recognized as the keynotes, but for all the color and the proportions there was something missing. The recesses were like empty frames. "They need the figure of a Francis I to complete them, or of a Diane de Poitiers, or even of a Henry III."

On the subject of Gaston d'Orléans's wing he was more opinionated.

This fine, frigid mansion [he calls it, before proceeding on a splendid generalized assault against the reputation of Mansart], whom a kind providence did not allow to make over the whole palace in the superior manner of his superior age. This had been a part of Gaston's plan—he was a blunderer born, and this precious project was worthy of him. This execution of it would surely have been one of the great misdeeds of history. Partially performed, the misdeed is not altogether to be regretted; for as one stands in the court of the castle, and lets one's eye wander from the splendid wing of Francis I—which is the last work of free and joyous invention—to the ruled lines and blank spaces of the ponderous pavilion of Mansart, one makes one's reflections upon the advantage, in even the least personal of the arts, of having something to say, and upon the stupidity of a taste which has ended by becoming an aggregation of negatives. Gaston's wing, taken by itself, has much of the *bel air* which was to belong to the architecture of Louis XIV; but, taken in contrast to its flowering, laughing, living neighbour, it marks the difference between inspiration and calculation.

So much for Mansart. James, representative of an age which did not value highly the pure lines and classical proportions of seventeenth-century architecture, would naturally have preferred the less balanced exuberance of François I's wing. And so it proved. "This exquisite, this extravagant, this transcendent piece of architecture is the most joyous utterance of the French Renaissance." The commanding feature, from which one cannot easily look away, is the staircase. It was built to impress by a King who adored flamboyance. "It forms a kind of chiselled cylinder, with wide interstices, so that the stairs are open to the air. Every inch of this structure, of its balconies, its pillars, its great central columns, is wrought over with lovely images, strange and ingenious devices, prime among which is the great heraldic salamander of Francis I. The salamander is everywhere at Blois—over the chimneys, over the doors, on the walls. This whole quarter bears the stamp of that eminently pictorial prince.".

One can still imagine the scene in the great courtyard as the King rode in from a day's hunting or there was a re-enactment of a medieval tournament. The window embrasures would have been crowded with courtiers, the staircase lit by flaming torches. François's Field of the Cloth of Gold was an evanescent extravagance. His château at Blois was beauty and reality combined.

Then, on the death of his wife, Claude de Bretagne, the building ceased, to be taken up again a century later. In between those two dates, the House of Valois would fall and the House of Bourbon would triumph. And the Duc de Guise and his brother the Cardinal de Lorraine would be assassinated. The whole episode has a bizarre inevitability about it, echoing perhaps the murder of Thomas à Becket at Canterbury, though there were few similarities between Henry Plantagent, Henry II of England, and the foppish, effeminate Henri III de Valois. It was never wise, however, to set oneself on a level with one's ruler (Wolsey had discovered this sad truth when he defied Henry VIII, and so would Nicolas Fouquet in the reign of Louis XIV, though by then quasi-judicial murder was somewhat more difficult to justify or explain away) and that was precisely what Henri de Guise had done. The wife of the Maréchal de Retz saw the point: "These Lorraines had such an air of distinction that alongside them the other princes looked plebeian." And as another contemporary observed: "The too great authority of the duc de Guise began to annoy not only the King, but all who loved the welfare, peace and quiet of the Realm."

Henri III was neither brave nor popular, but he was vindictive in his weakness. Once the idea of crushing forever the power of the Guises had been put in his mind, he prepared his plan with great speed. The deed would be done at Blois in the early morning of Friday, 23 December 1588. Guise himself received a number of warnings, but he ignored them. He was an arrogant man, utterly contemptuous of the King. He was also always surrounded by a strong bodyguard. But there was a flaw both in his argument and in his defense. Henri III, a consummate coward but a shrewd tactician, knew that the only place where his hated rival would be vulnerable was in the King's own apartments. The Spanish ambassador confirmed the weakness: "The one real danger to which he is exposed could only be in the Cabinet du Roi, where one is only admitted on one's own, and where this Prince would have every facility to have him attacked and killed."

Very rapidly, forty-five men, either loyal to the King or sufficiently bribed to appear so, were positioned in the King's apartments and on the staircase leading to them. The King had not slept, and frantically paced up and down. Guise continued to ignore all warnings and rose at six o'clock. The weather, according to an eyewitness, was "the most obscure, the darkest, the wettest" he had ever seen. One of the secretaries of state was sent to summon Guise to the royal presence, but the doorkeeper of the Council Chamber would not let him in. The secretary returned ashen-faced to the King, who ordered him to rub some color back into his cheeks before returning to the Council Chamber. This time he was allowed to enter. "Sir," he said to Guise, "the King is asking for you; he is in the Vieux Cabinet."

A few minutes later, Guise was dead, stabbed over and over again by eight assassins. Henri III had watched his enemy's death throes. Now he emerged from his hiding place and slapped Guise's face. "God, how large he is!" he was heard to say. "He seems even bigger now that he is dead than he was when he was alive." The Cardinal de Lorraine was murdered the following morning, on Christmas Eve, and the two dead bodies were burned and their remains thrown into the Loire.

The shadow of Henri de Guise is a long one. All the world loves a good murder, and how much more when the killer is of royal blood. Visitors to the château of Blois may look in admiration at Louis XII's simple but elegant brick and stone wing; they may marvel at the splendor of François I's staircase or smile at the recurring salamanders. But their attention will unswervingly be drawn to the scene of the Duc de Guise's assassination, each event in each room lovingly described, each supposed bloodstain gloatingly indicated. Let Henry James have the last word:

> All the old apartments have been rechristened, as it were; the geography of the castle has been re-established. The guard-rooms, the bedrooms, the closets, the oratories, have recovered their identity. Every spot connected with the murder of the Duke of Guise is pointed out by a small, shrill boy, who takes you from room to room, and who has learned his lesson in perfection. The place is full of Catherine de Medici, of Henry III, of memories, of ghosts, of echoes, of possible evocations and revivals. It is covered with crimson and gold. The fireplaces and the ceilings are magnificent; they look like expensive "sets" at the grand opera.

IN SEPTEMBER 1519, François I decided to commission "a beautiful and sumptuous edifice" at Chambord. His reason for choosing such an unsuitable marshy site is obscure. De la Saussaye spoke of a *"souvenir de premières amours,"* but as Henry James tartly pointed out it was certainly a very massive memento. Rather, it seems to have been, at least initially, a kind of mammoth hunting lodge, where François liked to escape with a group of close friends from the more ceremonial and rigid atmosphere of Blois. Like Louis XIV, with his single-minded interest in the building of Versailles (another highly unsuitable, equally marshy site, it will be remembered), François devoted both time and money to what, if the designs had been carried out down to the final intricate detail, would have been the most extraordinary architectural creation before the building of the Royal Pavilion at Brighton; and, indeed, the similarity between the two does not end there, for there is something oddly Oriental about the roof line of Chambord. Félibien, writing at the time, commented on the mixture of styles, which were neither Gothic nor modern, and was astonished at the number of pavilions, towers, and turrets. Henry James wrote about "a magnificent Orientalism" and continued: "The towers, the turrets, the cupolas, the gables, the lanterns, the chimneys, look more like the spires of a city than the salient points of a single building." And Vivian Rowe speaks of "the skyline of Constantinople on a single roof." Jerome Lippomano, who was told that the foundations alone had cost 300,000 francs, contented himself with a single sweeping sentence: "I have seen many magnificent buildings in my time, but never anything so beautiful or so rich as this."

Impressive it undoubtedly is, but whether Chambord is truly beautiful is a moot point. Is the grandeur not excessive, the setting too forbidding, the emptiness too glacial, the clutch of excrescences on the roof veering toward the preposterous? Cool and classical it certainly is not, but it appears almost as peculiar as Elizabeth I's palace of Nonesuch must have seemed a few decades later. It is more a candidate for the *Guinness Book of Records* than a fine building. The park surrounding it runs to nearly 14,000 acres. The château is 170 yards long and 120 deep. There are 440 rooms and heaven knows how many windows. There is a chimney for every day of the year, leap year not included, which strikes a mean note. The six towers are sixty feet in diameter. The roof is, in Ian Dunlop's phrase, an overcrowded chessboard. The great double spiral staircase rises to the lantern, which itself rises a further 108 feet. Vivian Rowe is balanced in his assessment: "It is very beautifully executed and decorated, but remains an architectural and (for the times) mathematical *tour de force* rather than a practical addition to the palace. It must have been little more than a showplace; after all, there are another sixty-two staircases for day to day use!" His point about the spiral staircase could equally be applied to the château as a whole.

The impression which I have always carried away with me, however, is one of emptiness. It does not seem to matter how many tourists are thronging its vast rooms, or how brightly the sun shines outside, the feeling of cold abandonment never leaves either the château or the visitor. It has always been so. As Ian Dunlop says, "It has perhaps been occupied one week for every year that it has stood empty." François soon tired of it. The Emperor Charles V paid a visit; Gaston d'Orléans lived there for a time; Louis XIV organized some *fêtes royales;* Louis XV's father-in-law, the former King of Poland, Stanislas Leczinski, was given Chambord as an official residence, but was driven out by the extreme cold of the winter and the feverish heat of the summer.

Only the Maréchal de Saxe seems, predictably, to have taken Chambord in his stride. Victor at the battle of Fontenoy, illegitimate scion of the House of Saxony, Maurice de Saxe was one of the most ebullient and colorful men in an age hardly renowned for insipid caution. He arrived at Chambord in 1748, and died there two years later. But they were noisy and enjoyable years. Saxe kept a private army, which included regiments of Uhlans and Tartars, as well as a private bodyguard of Negro soldiers mounted on white horses. He hunted, entertained lavishly, and continued his energetic pursuit of pretty women. He also drained the moat, though this seems to have had little effect. "Chambord," he wrote to a friend, "is a hospital. I have more than 300 sick, several dead, and the others have the look of exhumed corpses."

Just before the Revolution, the Englishman Arthur Young came to Chambord. He was unexpectedly impressed, greatly preferring it to Versailles, though he decided that it would be better suited to the cultivation of turnips. A few years later, his fantasy might have come true. The château, like so many other buildings at the time of the Revolution, was gutted, and it remained empty until it was presented to the infant Duc de Bordeaux, grandson of Charles X, last of the Bourbons. His toys, pathetic relics, are still on show.

When Henry James visited Chambord, he, too, was struck by the feeling of desolation. "The place was empty and silent; shadows of gargoyles, of extraordinary projections, were thrown across

the clear gray surfaces. One felt that the whole thing was mon-
strous. . . . Within, it is a wilderness of empty chambers, a royal
and romantic barrack." He failed to understand why François I
had chosen such a sandy, disagreeable place to build. Chambord
seemed to him unnecessary, stupid, lacking in history or interesting historical owners, eloquent only because it was a ruin. But, like
so many other visitors who are overwhelmed but rarely delighted,
he was prepared to admit that Chambord possessed *something*.

> On the whole, Chambord makes a great impression; and
> the hour I was there, while the yellow afternoon light slanted
> upon the September woods, there was a dignity in its desola-
> tion. It spoke, with a muffled but audible voice, of the van-
> ished monarchy, which had been so strong, so splendid, but
> to-day has become a sort of fantastic vision, like the cupolas
> and chimneys that rose before me. I thought, while I lingered
> there, of all the fine things it takes to make up such a mon-
> archy; and how one of them is a superfluity of mouldering,
> empty palaces. Chambord is touching—that is the best word
> for it.

THERE COULD BE no greater contrast than that between Chambord
and Cheverny. The former is huge, eccentric, and, above all, empty;
the latter is small, elegant, and, above all, lived in. Mademoiselle
de Montpensier, who had played with her father, Gaston d'Orléans, on Chambord's staircase, had no doubt which of the two
châteaux she preferred. "You were born in an enchanted palace,"
she wrote to the Marquise de Montglat, whose father had built
Cheverny. Henri Hurault had abandoned the old castle, perhaps
because it reminded him of his first wife's adulterous affair with
her page (the page, caught in flagrante, leaped from the bedroom
window, broke his leg and was killed by Hurault; the wife was said
to have been poisoned), and started the process of rebuilding in
the late 1620s. Cheverny was designed as a whole rather than as an
addition to a previous building. It is entirely successful. Ian Dunlop describes the basic layout: "Two massive end pavilions, each
crowned with an imperial dome and cupola; a narrow staircase in
the centre, surmounted by a pyramidal roof and belfry and two
symmetrical *corps de logis* uniting the pavilions, each with its separate high-pitched roof."

Symmetry is the key to the effect given by Cheverny. But it is not, as some observers maintain, an austere effect; it is, rather, perfect in a pure, uncomplicated way. And the interior is certainly far from austere. An early visitor to Cheverny, Elie Brackenhoffer, was impressed: "The house is neither vast nor large, but it has none the less good and beautiful apartments adorned with fine tapestries, good pictures and valuable furniture. In particular there is a gallery in which are to be seen full-length portraits, life-sized, of the most illustrious of our kings and notables; they are very well painted." Today the décor is equally rich, though many of the incidental touches have changed. By a miracle, and because of the courage, popularity, and sangfroid of the then owner, Dufort de Cheverny, Cheverny survived the Revolution more or less intact.

Henry James visited the château on the way back from Chambord to Blois. "The light had already begun to fade, and my drive reminded me of a passage in some rural novel by Madame Sand. I passed a couple of timber and plaster churches, which looked very old, black, and crooked, and had lumpish wooden porches and galleries encircling the base. By the time I reach Cheverny, the clear twilight had approached." He did not expect to be let in, but was ushered on by "a very tidy little portress." "I obeyed her to the letter, and my turn brought me into sight of a house as charming as an old manor in a fairy tale. I had but a rapid and partial view of Cheverny; but that view was a glimpse of perfection. A light, sweet mansion stood looking over a wide green lawn, over banks of flowers and groups of trees. It had a striking character of elegance, produced partly by a series of Renaissance busts let into circular niches in the façade. The place looked so private, so reserved, that it seemed an act of violence to ring, a stranger and foreigner, at the graceful door."

Ring he did, however. Perhaps it is because of the celebrity of Chambord, a tour of which takes some hours, but one seems invariably to come to Cheverny in the late afternoon. In the autumn, as the light fades, and the lamps are lit throughout the house, and the smell of dinner cooking seeps out from the kitchen, Cheverny seems even more than usual a private house, however grand. James had the same experience. "It was near the dinner-hour—the most sacred hour of the day; but I was freely conducted into the inhabited apartments. They are extremely beautiful. What I chiefly remember is the charming staircase of white embroidered stone, and the great *salle des gardes* and *chambre à coucher du roi* on the second floor. . . . The guardroom is a superb apartment. . . . The servant opened the shutters of a single window, and the last rays of the twilight slanted into the rich brown gloom. It was in the same picturesque fashion that I saw the bedroom (adjoining) of Henry IV, where a legendary-looking bed, draped in folds long unaltered, defined itself in the haunted dusk. Cheverny remains to me a very charming, a partly mysterious vision."

He drove back to Blois—"there was a damp autumnal smell and the occasional sound of a stirring thing"—with thoughts of François I and Henri IV. But he was wrong to think of kings. No monarch ever slept at Cheverny; the great bedroom was only there just in case. And that is possibly why Cheverny is so entrancing. For all the sumptuous decorations—Henry James would be amazed to see the change—Cheverny has none of the grandiosity and the pomp and circumstance which invest Blois and Chambord. It is a rich country gentleman's home, not just a house. A pack of hounds is maintained; the stables are occupied; the parterres and flower beds are looked after. It is all, perhaps, a little reminiscent of eighteenth-century England.

LA FONTAINE was succinct in his evaluation of the royal château of Amboise: *"Ce qu'il y a de beau, c'est la vue."* Charles VIII chose the site with great care. It was elevated, so that the air was fresher and cleaner; the hunting round about was extremely rich; and, above all, there was that view. No wonder Catherine de Medici, never easy to please, called Amboise "a residence so beautiful, so healthy and so convenient for the lodging of one's children."

Charles had been in Italy in 1495, and he returned with no less than twenty-two craftsmen and experts to help him create an Italianate palace. A gardener, a jeweler, an architect, a turner of alabaster, a specialist in marquetry, a builder of organs, a maker of architectural models, a goldsmith, a painter of ceilings, even "a subtle inventor for the incubation and hatching of chickens," they all traveled in the royal baggage train. The Renaissance was indeed born, though transmuted into something essentially French. François I continued the work abandoned when Charles died from a cerebral hemorrhage after cracking his head on a low door lintel. Leonardo da Vinci was invited to Amboise, and he lived at Le Clos-Lucé until his death in 1519.

François, ever eager to show off, invited the Emperor Charles V to Amboise in December 1539. Joachim du Bellay recorded the scene: "In order that the Emperor's arrival should be the more magnificent, the King ordained that it should be by night, by means of one of the said towers, adorned with every embellishment that could be devised, and so furnished with flambeaux and other lights that one could see as clearly as at high noon in the open country." It was a Renaissance equivalent to son et lumière, though the lumière turned out to be less than wholly satisfactory. "When the Emperor was half way up, a certain ill-fated torch-bearer set fire to it, so that the whole tower was in flames, and because of the tapestries which caught fire, the smoke was so dense, being unable to find an outlet, that there was great doubt but that the Emperor would suffocate." Chaos reigned. Charles may have suspected an attempt on his life. François felt humiliated and wanted to hang the incompetent torchbearer on the spot. Everyone staggered around until the smoke cleared. The culprit was pardoned on the Emperor's express wish. He may even have experienced some mild malicious pleasure at the whole ludicrous scene.

Twenty-one years later, Amboise would witness a far more bloodcurdling scene. François II now reigned, but he was still a boy, and real power lay in the hands of his mother Catherine de Medici and the Guise faction. A gentleman from Périgord, a Protestant, Godefroy de Barry, Seigneur de la Rénaudie, was determined to bring down Guise. He laid plans for an attack on Amboise. The whole thing went disastrously wrong. At first, the conspirators managed to create considerable alarm. The Spanish ambassador noted that "the terror was so great, there might have been an army at the gates of the Château." But the rebellious attacks on Amboise were quite uncoordinated and were dealt with effectively. La Rénaudie was killed during a skirmish, and the Guises decided the moment was ripe for revenge. It was made all too easy for them. The Spanish ambassador again: "It seems as if God has turned their minds; they [the rebels] allow themselves to be captured like children."

And once captured, they were exterminated in the most revolting way. They were hanged from the battlements, they were put into sacks and thrown alive into the Loire, they were broken on the wheel. And the Guises, the Royal Family, and the court watched. Régnier de la Planche observed the carnage. "In order the better to see the prisoners who had been given over to the cruellest torments, some still booted and spurred, some with body and limbs already broken on the wheel, some decapitated, the gentlemen in their silks and their velvets came and arranged themselves at the windows, with their ladies, as if it were some theatrical performance, without any sign of pity or compassion that was not feigned." The boy king looked on, his girl bride, the future Mary Queen of Scots, looked on. This was no Renaissance spectacle, it more resembled the worst excesses of the most degenerate Roman emperors. Only the Duchesse de Guise, the mother of Henri de Guise and the Cardinal de Lorraine, could watch no longer. She turned to Catherine de Medici as she left the balcony: "Such scenes revolt me. Never has a mother had more cause to feel afflicted. How great a storm of hatred and revenge is gathered over the heads of my unhappy sons." They were prophetic words.

Henry James, when he visited Amboise, overheard an English lady commenting on the château: "It is very, very dirty, but very curious." Between the departure of the French court in 1560—driven away by the stench of rotting corpses in the river and perhaps by their consciences—and the 1880s, Amboise hardly impinges on history. Somewhat bizarrely, Abd-el-Kader, the Arab leader who fought French colonial ambitions between 1832 and 1847, was imprisoned in the Salle des Etats, to be released after Napoleon III came to power. It was often a prison; it was often a barracks. The walls were defaced, no one could have visualized Amboise as a royal palace on which so many Italian craftsmen had lavished their art. Nevertheless James found much to admire: "The interior is virtually a blank, the old apartments having been chopped up into smaller rooms. . . . Denuded and disfeatured within, and bristling without with bricklayers' ladders, the place was yet extraordinarily impressive and interesting."

But once again it was what can be seen from the walls which caught James's fancy. "I should confess that we spent a great deal of time in looking at the view. Sweet was the view, and magnificent. . . . It seemed to us that we had never been in a place where there were so many points of vantage to look down from. In the matter of position Amboise is certainly supreme among the old houses of the Loire. . . . The platforms, the bastions, the terraces, the high-perched windows and balconies, the hanging gardens and dizzy crenellations, of this complicated structure, keep you in perpetual intercourse with an immense horizon."

The Italian gardens vanished, damage was done by German shells in 1940, further damage occurred in 1944, and over the centuries something like half the original château has vanished. But the immense horizon never changed.

It was from Amboise that Henry James and his companions—Fanny Kemble, the great actress, her son Owen, and her daughter Sarah—drove along the Loire to Chaumont. The expedition was not wholly successful. The woman who kept the inn at Amboise had assured them that the château was open, but on arrival at Chaumont they discovered that was not so, because the family who owned it were in residence. A series of negotiations with the lodge keeper ensued. "She tried to arrange a compromise, one of the elements of which was that we should descend from our carriage and trudge up a hill which would bring us to a designated point, where, over the paling of the garden, we might obtain an oblique and surreptitious view of a small portion of the castle walls." Fanny was not amused by the notion and remained in the carriage. (She seems, incidentally, to have behaved in a generally unadventurous way, even scorning a glass of sparkling Vouvray, merely because it was not champagne.)

James did not think that it was worth the detour. "It forms a vast, clean-scraped mass, with big round towers, ungarnished with a leaf of ivy or a patch of moss, surrounded by gardens of moderate extent . . . and looking rather like an enormously magnified villa." So much for one of the most beautiful châteaux in the whole of the Loire Valley. But James relented when, driving back across the Loire in order to take train to Tours, he caught a glimpse of Chaumont. "The towers, the pinnacles, the fair front of the château, perched above its fringe of garden and the rusty roofs of the village, and facing the afternoon sky, which is reflected also in the great stream that sweeps below—all this makes a contribution to your happiest memories of Touraine."

One feels, though, that he was damning Chaumont with faint praise. Perhaps Fanny Kemble's disapproval had affected his judgment. Mme de Staël, though, who lived at Chaumont during the summer of 1810, shared James's lack of appreciation. When asked by Benjamin Constant whether she did not admire the view, she responded dismissively: "I was thinking of Paris, and in truth I confess I prefer the black trickle that I see there to the clear and limpid waters of the Loire here." Mme de Staël's soul seems to have lacked a certain sense of poetry.

Perhaps she would have preferred the original château at Chaumont. It was demolished in 1465, on the orders of Louis XI. Five years earlier, Georges d'Amboise was born there. By the time of his death in 1510, the latter was Governor of Touraine and the King's Chamberlain; more important, he had restored both his family's standing and Chaumont. The new château was designed as a defensive castle and boasted a particularly impressive donjon, as well as a staircase which was almost the prototype for François I's staircase at Blois. In the sixteenth century, Diane de Poitiers, Henri II's mistress, was forced to give up Chenonceaux and move to Chaumont. The north side was altered, and by the middle of the eighteenth century it had totally vanished, leaving the two gatehouse towers and the drawbridge which can be seen today.

By 1875, Chaumont was in a state of almost total disrepair. Then the Prince and Princesse de Broglie moved in, and considerable improvements were put in hand. Unfortunately, their money ran out, and it was even thought it would be necessary to get rid of an elephant which had been presented to the Broglies by the Maharajah of Kapurthala and had a prodigious appetite. The elephant was, however, retained, and a ban placed instead on the consumption of foie gras sandwiches at tea. One wishes that Henry James and the elephant had met. But at least he might have agreed with a pronouncement made by another Prince de Broglie: "He who has not seen the sun set at Chaumont has not experienced one of nature's most lovely spectacles."

CHENONCEAUX (OR CHENONCEAU, as the purists prefer) is surely the most beautiful of all the châteaux of the Loire. Its setting is, of course, unique, and as a consequence its design. Few architects would have had the genius to build on the long gallery actually over the river Cher. It is the water flowing through those supporting, exquisitely proportioned arches that gives that extraordinary impression of grace and fluidity, as if the whole château might at any moment float downstream. The entrance façade is fine enough, with its drawbridge and splendid formal gardens, but it is the side view which takes the breath away.

The château was originally built by a family called Bohier, rich but not noble. Perhaps it was too beautiful, certainly the fortunes of the family crashed disastrously, in any event Chenonceaux was possessed on behalf of François I in 1536. He visited it on only two occasions. He died on 31 March 1547. Three months later, his successor Henri II's favorite mistress, Diane de Poitiers, moved in. But as soon as Henri was dead, his widow Catherine de Medici ousted Diane, and Chenonceaux's greatest period began. The gallery was built on top of Philibert de l'Orme's bridge across the Cher; the library was created; the park laid out; and the château filled with the finest furniture and tapestries.

Chenonceaux continued to remain in royal hands. Henri III's widow was there when the news of her husband's death came, and there she remained. The château's interior was painted black throughout, all color was removed, and Queen Louise moved sadly about in the deepest mourning, white rather than black because of her royal blood. In 1598, the château was made over to her niece, and for some time a community of Capuchin nuns lodged there.

Then, in 1733, Louise-Marie-Madeleine Dupin moved in to Chenonceaux. The daughter of one of the richest men in France, she brought the money to restore the house; but she also brought impeccable taste, an irreproachable reputation, and the art of making friends. Henry James was most approving. "The best society that ever assembled there was collected at Chenonceaux during the middle of the eighteenth century. . . . The sixty years that preceded the French Revolution were the golden age of fireside talk and of those pleasures which proceed from the presence of women in whom the social art is both instinctive and acquired. The women of that period were, above all, good company; the fact is attested by a thousand documents. Chenonceaux offered a perfect setting to free conversation; and infinite joyous discourse must have mingled with the liquid murmur of the Cher."

Even that old curmudgeon Jean Jacques Rousseau was inclined to give it his seal of approval. "In 1747," he says in his *Confessions,* "we went to spend the autumn in Touraine, at the Château of Chenonceaux. . . . We amused ourselves greatly in this fine spot; the living was of the best, and I became as fat as a monk." Half a century later, Mme Dupin, now a very old lady, showed a visitor around the château. She led him to the room where Rousseau had once slept. "There, young man," she said, "is the cave of the bear from Geneva."

Chenonceaux was quite untouched by the Revolution. A mild attempt at destruction was averted by the reminder that there was the only bridge crossing the Cher for miles. In the nineteenth century, Mme Pelouze stripped away certain encrustations, and in the twentieth the Menier family used the profits from their chocolate empire to maintain the château in all its glory.

When Henry James visited Chenonceaux, he was somewhat startled to encounter an old acquaintance, the gondolier Checco, whom he had last met in Venice. (The romantic novelist Marie Corelli would later import a Venetian gondolier to the even more improbable setting of Stratford-upon-Avon.) But the sideways view of the château along the Cher banished all sense of incongruity. "This was the right perspective; we were looking across the river of time. The whole scene was deliciously mild. The moon came up; we passed back through the gallery and strolled about a little longer in the gardens. It was very still." There was time for an excellent dinner at Le Bon Laboureur (James called it Le Grand Monarque, a name which it had ceased to bear since the Revolution), and they were off back to Tours once again.

Le Bon Laboureur still has a first-class restaurant, and the village of Chenonceaux retains its charm against the tourist buses and container trucks which sweep through far too fast. The château is perhaps a trifle too glossy in its presentation, with baroque music echoing down the gallery and spectacular son et lumière. But its sheer beauty is unimpaired. And I look back to my first visit and hear Madame telling me that Chenonceaux was in a peculiarly odd situation during the Second World War; that one bank of the Cher was in German-occupied territory, and the other was in Vichy France. The gallery, perhaps because it was so dazzling, was a kind of aquatic-cum-architectural no-man's-land. The thought might have amused Catherine de Medici.

WITH THE ABLE assistance of Mr. Henry James, six great châteaux of the Loire have been displayed, their history, their architecture, and, perhaps most important, the effect they make. Blois, Chambord, Cheverny, Amboise, Chaumont, Chenonceaux: there would probably be little argument about this representative sextet. But in many ways the most delightful châteaux are the smaller, more private, less grandiloquent ones. The marvelous moated settings of Azay-le-Rideau and Sully-sur-Loire, the domed roofs of Serrant and Valençay, which are so striking after such a multitude of *poivrières,* the imposing ensemble of Chinon, the beautiful entrance gates at Montgeoffroy, the pleasures of Champigny and Brissac, Le Plessis-Bourré and Chanteloup, Le Lude and Richelieu, even the somewhat debased splendors of Tours, which appears to have suffered far more fundamentally from modern road traffic than it ever did from the fighting of the Second World War: all these would be considered in the very first rank in any other region of France. And then there are the smaller manor houses like Beauregard and Boumois, with their weathered walls, glowing gardens, and almost invariable dovecotes.

Here, I think, we arrive at the essential relevance to France of the Loire Valley, not only of the Loire itself, but of the other rivers, the Loir, the Indre, the Cher, and the Cisse, and of the châteaux built along the banks. The area was once called the cradle of the kings of France, though the reference was almost exclusively to the Valois dynasty. France's destiny was worked out, often bloodily, in one of the most ravishing countrysides one could ever hope to come upon. Religious and dynastic quarrels reached fever pitch against Henry James's "immense horizon." But the murders and revenges and brutalities are less important than one inescapable fact. Here, at Blois and Amboise and Chenonceaux, the French—indeed the European—Renaissance occurred, and nothing was ever the same again.

viii

Capable de Tout

RANÇOIS-MARIE AROUET was born in Paris in 1694 and lived the greater part of his life at Ferney near Geneva in Switzerland. He died in 1778. He was twenty-one at the death of Louis XIV. His death preceded the French Revolution by a mere eleven years. He epitomized the best qualities of the eighteenth century. He was the quintessential French genius—sane, witty, compassionate, politically alert, a spinner of tales and fables, and yet a distinguished historian. He hated repression and humbug and religious cant. He never lost his sense of humor, his elegance and style. We know him as Voltaire.

Certain writers represent certain national characteristics. It is always a dangerous game to play; it is far too easy to force square pegs into hastily adapted holes. Thus Rabelais, Ronsard, Racine, Rousseau, Baudelaire, Balzac, Flaubert, Zola, and even Victor Hugo *hélas*—the list is ad lib—all of them can be said to have encapsulated in their works a particular aspect of the French character. In the case of Voltaire, he formed opinion rather than reflected it, he imposed rather than mirrored. Larousse is instructive in its analysis. After granting him an *"esprit hardi et curieux et d'une merveilleuse souplesse"* ("fearless, curious, wonderfully subtle wit"), the potted biography proceeds to assess his unique qualities: "His literary and social influence was enormous, as much through the energy which he used to defend the causes which seemed to him just against religious intolerance, as through the essential character of his works: no writer, in fact, was more *French* in the limpidity, the elegance, the witty precision and the purity of style; no man at the same time was more *human* in the general inclination of the philosophical thought which permeates all his works: respect for the conscience and the liberty of the individual, an unshakable belief in progress."

Voltaire's literary output was formidable. Over the space of sixty years he wrote more than ten thousand letters; two great histories, on the ages of Louis XIV and of Charles XII of Sweden; epic poems; tragedies (according to Byron, when asked why no woman had ever written a tolerable tragedy, Voltaire replied, "Ah, the composition of a tragedy requires *testicles*," a rare example of prejudice on his part); novels and stories, of which *Candide* is the most celebrated; lyric poetry; and great quantities of philosophy, in particular the *Lettres Philosophiques* and the *Dictionnaire Philosophique*. Houdon's great bust of Voltaire shows a witty, worldly quicksilver mind behind the amused, cynical face. He was certainly far too clever for even such a tolerant man as the Duc d'Orléans, the French Regent, let alone for less discerning aristocrats who considered that a sound thrashing in public was the best treatment for insolence. He was too clever for London society, though it was in England that he developed his theories on freedom and religious bigotry. He was too clear-sighted to be taken in by Frederick the Great's liberal protestations, though the realization provided one of the most bitter disappointments of his life.

Appalling disasters moved him unusually in a hard age not

given to sentimentality. The earthquake which destroyed Lisbon convinced him that God was by no means synonymous with good. The fatuous attempts by the philosopher Leibnitz to persuade people that all was for the best in the best of all possible worlds received short shrift at Voltaire's hands in his devastating fable *Candide*. He was equally shocked by the hypocrisy of the English when they executed Admiral John Byng after the loss of Minorca to the French, *"pour encourager les autres,"* as he was by the barbaric breaking on the wheel of the Huguenot Jean Calas, who had been falsely accused of murdering his son in order to stop him from recanting and returning to the Catholic faith. In *L'Ingénu,* he wrote: "Indeed, history is nothing more than a tableau of crimes and misfortunes."

But he was not content to shed tears over the dead, the abused, the persecuted. In a famous letter to d'Alembert in 1762, he nailed his colors to the mast: "Whatever you do, stamp out abuses, and love those who love you"—*"écrasez l'infâme"* ("crush what is infamous"), one of the bravest phrases in French literature, to be mirrored by Emile Zola with his *"J'accuse."* And it was Voltaire who was credited with another celebrated challenge to the forces of reaction: "I disapprove of what you say, but I will defend to the death your right to say it."

The anger and the passion are explicit. So, too, are the elegance and the wit, the purity of language, which so delighted the biographer in Larousse and indeed all right-thinking Frenchmen. *"Le secret d'ennuyer est . . . de tout dire"* ("The best way of boring people is . . . to say everything"); *"Si Dieu n'existait pas, il faudrait l'inventer"* ("If God did not exist, one would have to invent Him"); *"Dieu n'est pas pour les gros bataillons, mais pour ceux qui tirent le mieux"* ("God is on the side not of the big battalions but of those who shoot the best"): these maxims are indeed both elegantly phrased and wittily conceived.

Voltaire was suspicious of chauvinism. In a letter to Catherine the Great he poked fun at a *dame de la cour* at Versailles who was supposed to have declared, "What a shame about all that business at the tower of Babel which produced all the different languages; otherwise everyone would have spoken nothing but French." And he was remarkably free-thinking in his attitude toward sex. He considered it one of the great superstitions that virginity could ever be a virtue, and pursued the theme in a letter to a M. Mariott: "It amuses me that everyone should make a virtue out of the vice of chastity; and it's an odd sort of chastity which leads men straight to the sin of Onan, and girls to losing their color."

He could be as practical as Machiavelli in his consideration of politics and statecraft. There is nothing starry-eyed about one maxim, often borrowed by politicians, seldom with acknowledgment: "Governments need both shepherds and butchers." And there is nothing remotely utopian about *Candide*. Voltaire's previous *contes*, *Zadig* and *Micromégas*, had been comparatively good-natured and sunny. In *Candide*, the satire is intended to bite deep. Blind optimism is shown to be perverse and futile. The ridiculous homespun philosopher Pangloss parrots on about all being for the best in the best of all possible worlds. Disasters rain down. Earthquakes, shipwrecks, floggings, mutilation, war, disease, and death follow one another with the merest intervals for reconciliation and rediscovery; then off again Candide, Cunégonde, and Pangloss go, meeting nothing but prejudice, mental anguish, and physical agony. When Candide despairs of ever finding peace and quiet, all his valet Cacambo can suggest is to follow a river and trust to providence, on the curious basis that "even if we don't find anything agreeable, we will at least find something new."

At the end of *Candide*, the reader is left with three pieces of advice. The philosopher Martin proclaims that the only way to make life bearable is to work without reasoning. Pangloss insists on his theory of a chain of events leading to happiness: "All events are linked in the best of all possible worlds: because after all if you had not been chased out of the castle with the baron's boot delivering a series of kicks to your behind, all for the love of Mademoiselle Cunégonde, if you had not been handed over to the Inquisition, if you had not run from one end of America to the other, if you had not given the baron a good thrust of your sword, if you had not lost all your sheep in Eldorado, you would not be sitting here eating crystallised pine-kernels and pistachio nuts." To which the hapless Candide can only respond: "That is well said, but we must cultivate our garden."

To cultivate his garden, merely to attend to his own affairs, was the very last thing with which Voltaire would have been content. He was a man of action through words, a destroyer of shibboleths rather than a tilter at windmills. He once said that "superstition sets the whole world in flames," but added that "philosophy quenches them." He was supremely rational and clinical, but never eschewed passion. He did not suffer reputations gladly, maintaining that though respect was owed to the living, the dead were owed only truth. To read *Candide,* even when the irony has worn thin from repetition, is always a delight because it is such a model of pace and effect.

France in the eighteenth century was not short of men of genius: Diderot, Rousseau, d'Alembert, Montesquieu. But they were primarily thinkers, influential, of course, but very much of their age. Voltaire opened men's minds to the iniquities and in-equities of society as few others have in the history of the world. He could be violent in his denunciations, but he knew when wit and subtlety should be used, the rapier rather than the bludgeon. In retrospect, he seldom seems to have been wrong, perhaps because he welcomed progress and new ideas. He appears very modern. He also appears very French, as Larousse says.

Voltaire once used a somewhat mystifying phrase: *"Habacuc était capable de tout."* Habakkuk's capabilities may be shrouded in doubt, but it is quite certain that Voltaire himself was indeed capable of everything.

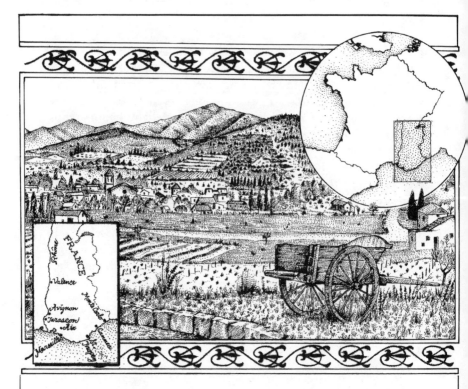

South

PROVENCE IS a country to which I am always returning, next week, next year, any day now, as soon as I can get on to a train. Here in London it is an effort of will to believe in the existence of such a place at all. But now and again the vision of golden tiles on a round southern roof, or of some warm, stony, herb-scented hillside will rise out of my kitchen pots with the smell of a piece of orange peel scenting a beef stew." We all need a taste or a smell that conjures up some hazy, unfocused memory. Though there is nothing unfocused about Provence. Here the light is sharp, the sun is hot, the colors are primary, the sensations are immediate. And like Elizabeth David, we thin-blooded Anglo-Saxons need to be coaxed back to life by the seductive heat of the South.

Ford Madox Ford, who loved France, and above all loved Provence, has a famous passage, exaggerated and idiosyncratic like so many of his assertions, which nevertheless contains a wholly acceptable truth: "Somewhere between Vienne and Valence, below Lyons on the Rhône, the sun is shining and south of Valence Provincia Romana, the Roman Province, lies beneath the sun. Then there is no more any evil, for there the apple will not flourish and the brussels sprout will not grow at all." Certainly, as the train leaves the station at Lyons, you feel a prick of excitement as the landscape begins to change, as the pines and olive trees and terraces of vines lie baking outside the window, as the smell of lavender and tuberose and thyme seems to permeate the compartment. The pace of life calms, the languor of lotus land steals over you, visions of Mediterranean fish grilling over bunches of fennel, of fat black olives and curiously shaped tomatoes, of cool bottles of tart pink wine, swirl up. The South has claimed another victim, and a willing one.

It is, of course, absurd to approach Provence except by train. If you arrive, *tout court,* at Nice airport, all the incidental, the essential, pleasures have been clinically excised. The shock of the new is poor compensation for those missed delights on the route down the Rhône Valley from Lyons and on to Marseilles. Each station evokes a memory, a literary connection, a culinary image: Arles, Avignon, Orange, Nîmes, Aix, Tarascon. Popes and troubadours, tragic heroines and comic heroes, Roman centurions and Impressionist painters seem to spring out from the Provençal landscape. The backcloth itself vibrates with color: the glowing red of the roof tiles, the bleached bone-white of the rocks which Cézanne so miraculously caught, the stark green of the umbrella pines, the scarlet and yellow of the canna lilies, the purple bougainvillea, the intense blue of the sky and the sea, away in the distance, glimpsed through the gray olive trees and the black cypresses.

This extraordinary palette spills over into the basic ingredients of everyday life. Stroll through the market of any small Provençal town, preferably one near the Mediterranean, and the colors seem to leap out. The grapes are stygian purple, the *primeurs* impossibly green, the pinks and silvers of the fish have escaped from a Chardin still life, the scarlet and black of the tomatoes and aubergines put a new gloss on Stendhal's title *The Red and the Black* (and Stendhal traveled extensively in the South of France), the carnations and gladioli and lilies on the flower stalls clash and riot. Perhaps, one thinks, it is the sun which imposes this extra layer of pigment. But Madame Léon Daudet found quite as much color in a simple meal indoors. "I know of nothing more appetising, on a very hot day, than to sit down in the cool shade of a dining-room with drawn Venetian blinds, at a little table laid with black olives, *saucisson d'Arles,* some fine tomatoes, a slice of water melon and a pyramid of little green figs baked by the sun."

It is time, though, to leave the generalized and to attack the particular, by means of a circuitous journey through Provence, following very roughly indeed the railway line from Lyons to the Italian border, a haphazard, eccentric tour which omits much that should be described and includes certain enthusiasms that may baffle the reader.

WE SHOULD START, perhaps, with Valence, if only because Ford Madox Ford tells us that that is the real *portail* to the South. In March 1838, Stendhal, who was at the time ostensibly French consul in Civitavecchia, though he does not seem to have taken his duties particularly seriously, set off on a four-month visit to the southern part of France. He commenced his journey in Bordeaux and traveled through Toulouse, Bayonne, Pau, Montpellier, Marseilles, Toulon, and Cannes. He reached Valence on 1 June. He was not impressed.

"Valence is a sordid town and, above all, paved with nasty little pointed stones not filled in with sand, which makes walking a serious problem to which you must give all your attention." He strongly advised the chief magistrate to plant some plane trees ("The Frenchman of the old school has no liking for natural beauties, whereas the Englishman's love of nature is his real delight, next only to his instinct to fight obstacles and never to forget his rank"), admired a bust of Pope Pius VI in the church of Saint Apollinaire ("He looks commonplace. Very good likeness"), thought most of the public buildings absurd, but approved the bridge over the Rhône.

Today, Valence, like Vienne, has a pleasantly provincial air, some handsome buildings, improved perhaps by the patina of age, and one renowned restaurant. But it is not essentially southern. It peers toward the south, but its feet are still planted fair and square in the center of France.

With Tarascon there is no such doubt. It is thoroughly Provençal. It does not possess the grandeur of Avignon, the elegance of Aix, or the important Roman buildings of Nîmes and Arles, but it has one claim to fame which not one of its more impressive neighbors possesses: It is inescapably linked with the eponymous hero of Alphonse Daudet's novel, one of those exceedingly rare comic French novels. Tartarin de Tarascon is an amalgam of the Grossmiths' Mr. Pooter in *Diary of a Nobody* and Conan Doyle's Brigadier Gerard. He is a boaster, an exaggerator, some would say a liar. He himself is aware of the possible accusation, and refutes it categorically through his creator's lips. Daudet is recorded as having posed a rhetorical question: "Is it fair to call a man a liar, who intoxicates himself with his own talk, who, without any low motive, without a thought of deception, of guile, of profit, tries to beautify his own existence and that of others with stories which he knows to be imaginary, but would like to be true or probable? . . . Besides, among men of the Midi nobody is deceived. Each privately corrects the falsified proportions. It is all a matter of reduction to the proper terms."

There is a superb irony to all this self-justification. Not only was Tartarin himself invented, but so was the Tarascon where he was supposed to have lived. The sad, funny truth is that Daudet merely liked the sound of Tarascon, the word had a euphonious, rather bragging air to it, so he borrowed it, and bestowed it on a small town which in reality lay fifteen miles on the other side of the Rhône. The real inhabitants of the real Tarascon were not amused. One family sued, others threatened retribution of a more immediate nature, the book itself was banned locally and for many years was unobtainable. Later, inevitably, the pendulum swung violently in the opposite direction, and the real Tarasconnais became ever more certain that Daudet had indeed written about their town. The tourist industry benefited, and still benefits.

Tartarin himself is a marvelous creation, full of boasts and braggadocio, swaggering about the place with a tall story ever at the ready, planning an absurd hunting expedition to Algeria in pursuit of lions, and getting himself into the mood by slaughtering any inoffensive bird which might have the temerity to fly across his path (though, as it transpires, his targets are often rather more unusual). His ambition is nicely summed up in Daudet's description of Tartarin's gardens: "Every plant was exotic: nothing but gums, calabash trees, cotton-woods, mangoes, banana-palms, date-palms, prickly pears, cacti, Indian figs. You would have thought yourself thirty thousand miles from Tarascon, in the heart of central Africa. None of these plants, of course, were their natural size. The coconut palms were hardly bigger than beetroots, and the baobab tree (*arbos gigantea*—the giant) was easily contained by a mignonette pot."

But it is the celebrated cap-shooting scene which is the essence of Tartarin, besides saying much on the subject of the Provençal as Nimrod. Daudet sets the scene:

> In the first place you must know that everyone down there, great and small, is a Sportsman. Shooting has been a passion in those parts since those mythological days when Tarasque, the local dragon, flourished her tail in the town marshes and the inhabitants of the day organised drives against her. That, as you may guess, was a long time ago.
>
> So every Sunday morning the whole of Tarascon takes up arms and leaves its gates, game-bag on back and gun in hand, with a straining of dogs and ferrets, and a clatter of bugles and hunting-horns. It is a superb sight. But unfortunately there is no game, absolutely none. Animals may be very stupid. But, as you can imagine, they finally took fright. For fifteen miles round Tarascon, burrows were empty, and nests forsaken. Not a blackbird, not a quail, not the tiniest leveret or so much as a sparrow.
>
> The hills around Tarascon, with their scent of myrtle, lavender and rosemary, are very tempting; and those fine muscat grapes bursting with sweetness that grow along the banks of the Rhône, are devilish appetising too. But on the other side is Tarascon and in the little world of fur and feather Tarascon has a very bad reputation. The very birds of passage have put a great cross against it on their route-maps, and when the wild duck, flying towards the Camargue in their long V-shaped formations, see the town's spires from afar, the leader gives a loud cry of "Tarascon! there is Tarascon." And the whole flight swerves away.

A solution must be found. So, every Sunday in the season (and, one expects, outside it, too) is given over to a ritual and lavish picnic, followed by a competition of cap shooting. Tartarin is far and away the most proficient at this peculiar form of exercise, and it is because his own cap is always in tatters by the end of Sunday that he is held in such esteem by the others.

The French attitude toward shooting and hunting is idiosyncratic and all-embracing. Being more interested in his stomach than in any sentimental feelings about song- as opposed to game-birds, and not allowing such matters as the breeding season to deflect him from his normal pursuits, the Provençal continues to shoot and snare as long as there is something around. Sophisticated and worldly Parisians find this single-minded passion barely credible and dismiss the Daudet account as long out of date. They are rather more shaken by Marcel Pagnol's boyhood memory: "A snare set in a terebinth guarantees the capture of a warbler, a thrush, a greenfinch, a blackbird. . . . We would place them as we climbed towards the heights all through the morning, then our quartet would stop for lunch near a spring, in the luminous shadow of a pine-tree. . . . Sometimes Uncle Jules would suddenly snatch up his gun and, with his mouth full, aim skywards through the branches at something nobody else had seen: and a wood-pigeon, an oriole, a sparrow-hawk would suddenly drop from the sky."

AVIGNON IS best seen from across the Rhône, perhaps from a window in Philip the Fair's huge, uncompromising tower which he built almost as a symbol of the French Crown's power over the Papal court. From Villeneuve-les-Avignon one has what the guidebook Michelin would call a panorama: the river itself, the old bridge of Saint Bénézet with its diminutive chapel and nursery-rhyme associations, and beyond the Palais des Papes, an extraordinary collection of towers and spires.

Villeneuve itself was once an important town, first strategically, later on account of the various summer palaces built by the cardinals in order to escape the heat and constriction of Avignon, above all because of the great Carthusian monastery and the Fort of Saint André, yet another indication of the French King's supremacy. After the dispersal of the Papal court, Villeneuve inevitably fell into decay. What time failed to achieve, the spirit of revolution hastened. In the middle of the nineteenth century, when the state turned its attention to the condition of ancient monuments, it was discovered that the Gothic tomb of Innocent VI was being used as a rabbit hutch. And by the beginning of the twentieth century, one English visitor could reel back aghast at the decay and collapse:

> The town of Villeneuve, that lies below the fortress, sadly belies its name, for a more concentrated collection of crumbling ruins could hardly be imagined. The Monastery of the Chartreuse . . . was for more than four hundred years one of the most important and prosperous in Languedoc. The walls enclosing it measure nearly a mile in circumference, and now its ruins form a squalid little town inhabited by over five hundred human beings, to say nothing of the domestic animals. The walls of its crumbling church are fast disappearing, the roof lets more than daylight in, and what little of it remains affords but a poor shelter for a few rickety, cumbrous, mud-stained carts and piles of faggots stored for winter use.

Now Villeneuve is recovering. The Carthusian monastery is being restored, and Philip the Fair's massive fort is beset by tourists. But the atmosphere of the place is somnolent, quite different from that of Avignon, so close but seemingly divided from the modern world by the breadth of the Rhône. In Avignon, all is bustle and movement and color. The cafés are full, as they have always been. A. S. Forrest expatiated on this peculiarly French phenomenon in the Edwardian era: "In summer, when the heat of the brilliant day gives place to the lovely glow of the Provençal evening, all Avignon sits outside around the tables that trespass in careless fashion upon the pavements. . . . The scene on a summer evening in the Place de l'Hôtel de Ville in Avignon is but a repetition on a smaller scale of what may be seen on any evening from one year's end to the other in the Cannebière at Marseilles, or farther distant still, across the Mediterranean in the Place du Gouvernement in the French city of Algiers."

Serious people do not, of course, come to Avignon for the cafés or restaurants (in my opinion, they should, particularly if they have the luck to dine at Hiély, one of the best restaurants in the whole of France); they come for the summer festival of music and the arts, above all for the history. The Palace of the Popes is certainly history writ large, since it records the most bizarre series of events ever to galvanize the successors to Saint Peter.

In 1305, Bertrand de Got, Archbishop of Bordeaux, succeeded Boniface VIII, and was crowned as Clement V. The new Pope was the inheritor of a state of utter chaos. Rome was not far short of anarchy, the whole of Italy was being ravaged by the endless wars between the Guelphs and the Ghibellines, and Philip the Fair of France was refusing to pay his taxes. Clement, who owned some property on the banks of the Rhône, decided to transport the entire Papal court to Avignon. The so-called Babylonian Captivity of the Papacy had begun. Seven popes would reign between 1309 and 1376, all of them Frenchmen. The independence and authority of the Church were undermined, and the influence of the Papacy throughout Europe severely weakened. Ahead lay the Great Schism, and a rising tide of doubt concerning the supremacy, indeed the infallibility, of the Pope in political and spiritual matters.

Clement V elected to live in the Dominican convent at Avignon, and his successor, John XXII, declined to move out of the Bishop's Palace. It was the third Pope of the Captivity, Benedict XII, who seemed to recognize the permanence of Avignon as the seat of the Papacy by rebuilding the Old Palace. Benedict was a Cistercian, and consequently his preference was for the plain and austere. The Old Palace resembles a castle or fortress, whereas the New Palace, built by Clement VI, is more properly palatial.

It was during the reign of Clement VI that Avignon became to all intents and purposes a capital city. The Pope acquired the town and the surrounding territory from Jeanne des Baux, Comtesse de Provence. It cost him 80,000 ducats, and the absolution of Jeanne from her supposed involvement in the murder by strangulation of her husband, Andrew of Hungary. It was a time of license and licentiousness. Petrarch was devasting in his condemnation: "Avignon is an abode of sorrows, the shame of mankind, a sink of vice . . . a sewer where all the filth of the universe has gathered. There God is held in contempt, money is worshipped, and the laws of God and man are trampled underfoot. Everything there breathes a lie; the air, the earth, the houses and above all the bedrooms."

Clement did not set a good example. One of his suspected

mistresses, the Comtesse de Turenne, "as rapacious as she was handsome, unblushingly sold positions and preferments procured by her ascendancy." Clement himself was described as "a fine gentleman, a prince munificent to profusion, a patron of the arts, but no saint," and under his reign Avignon attracted an extraordinary mixture of prelates and whores, merchants and chroniclers, heretics and cardinals, criminals and ambassadors. "Excited crowds would jostle to receive the Papal blessing and to see him when he rode abroad on his white mule, or to gape at such spectacles as Queen Jeanne, in a flowered robe and blue mantle, landing from the galley which had brought her from Naples, mounting her white palfrey and riding up to the Palace with eight cardinals in attendance."

Clement VI died in 1352, and under his successors a reaction to the splendors and immorality of his reign set in. Finally, in 1377, Gregory XI was prevailed upon by Saint Catherine of Siena to return to Rome. The Babylonian Captivity was at an end. The Great Schism began. A number of cardinals refused to leave Avignon and elected Robert, Cardinal of Geneva, as Clement VII. Rome and Avignon entered into a war of verbal attrition, waged with particular vehemence by the next Antipope, the Spaniard Peter de Luna, who ruled as Benedict XIII. Charles V of France decided that military action was the only choice. His troops laid siege to Avignon, but Benedict refused to capitulate. "He destroyed one of the arches of the Pont St. Bénézet to cut off the approaches from the river; and from the battlements and towers of his castle directed the engines of war with his own hands on the town and townsfolk, who suffered so severely that over a hundred houses and four thousand of the inhabitants were destroyed during the siege."

In April 1399, the siege was lifted. Benedict made various empty promises and was kept virtually under house arrest. Four years later, he was smuggled out of Avignon to Château Reynard in Provence. The internecine struggle between the popes in Rome and the antipopes in exile dragged on (at one time there was even an antipope to the antipope) while councils and conclaves attempted vainly to restore the unity of the Church. It was not until 1430 that a synod at Tortosa re-established the single Papacy. One hundred and twenty years had passed since Clement V had arrived in Avignon.

Nothing in the subsequent history of Avignon can possibly seem so dramatic as those events which threatened to destroy the Western Church. The town suffered during the French Revolution. There was an appalling massacre in 1791, another in 1795. But it was the White Terror of 1815 which set a new record in brutality. The restoration of the Bourbons after the fall of Napoleon was the sign for a settling of old scores. Totally innocent people were murdered, as the self-styled White Penitents went about their business, roaming as far as Marseilles in their quest for vengeance.

Avignon was the scene of a particularly appalling episode. Marshal Guillaume Brune was staying at the Hôtel de la Poste, on his way to Paris in order to appear before the new government.

> The news of his arrival had spread along with sinister stories as to his doings during the Revolution of 1789, and a great mob assembled around the hotel, broke in and shot the Marshal in cold blood. His body was on its way to burial when the crowd forced the bearers to change their course and proceed to the river-side, where a wooden bridge spanned the river. From this they threw the body of the Marshal into the silent Rhône. The ribald crowd fired shots into the body as it floated down the stream, a proceeding which they termed "military honours." On the arch of the bridge they wrote "The Tomb of Marshal Brune."

AIX. A TOWN of fountains and plane trees and fine houses. Mirabeau married and divorced there. Zola went to the lycée. So did Cézanne, who, more than any other painter, has caught the unique effect of heat on a landscape. So, too, did Darius Milhaud, who would introduce jazz rhythms into his conception of the world's creation and the plangent sadness of the Brazilian *saudades* into his piano pieces.

In *Map of Another Town*, M. F. K. Fisher offers an introduction:

> The town was put on its feet by a Roman whose elegant bathing place still splutters out waters, tepid to hot and slightly stinking, for a ceaseless genteel flow of ancient countesses and their consorts and a quiet dogged procession of arthritic postal clerks and Swiss bankers and English spinsters

suffering from indefinable malaises usually attributed to either their native climates or their equally native diets. This spa, more ancient than anyone who could possibly stay in it except perhaps I myself, is at the edge of the Old Town, at the head of the Cours Sextius, and more than one good writer has generated his own acid to etch its strange watery attraction.

Countless poems have been written too, in wine rather than acid, and countless pictures have been painted, about the healing waters and the ever-flowing fountains of the place. They will continue as long as does man, and the delicate iron balconies will cling to the rose-yellow walls, and if anyone else, from 200 B.C. to now, ever marked the same places on the map, in acid or wine or even tears, his reasons would not be mine. That is why Aix is what it is.

Aix is almost impossibly unlike other Provençal towns. There is heat, but it is mitigated by the splashing of the fountains, and by the four rows of plane trees which arch over the Cours Mirabeau. Marcel Renébon, in his book on Provence, waxed appropriately lyrical about this remarkably beautiful street. "Aix is nobility itself. It gives to the least plane-tree the grandeur of a cedar. On the Cours Mirabeau, where the song of the fountains mingles with Mozart's music, its good taste comes so naturally that not even the students can disturb it. It was the last city of France to give up its sedan chairs." Fisher, who is totally in love with the place, adds a glowing portrait.

> The Cours has teased poets and painters with its ineffable allure for more than three hundred years, but words and lines and colours do not capture the reasons why it is beautiful and not pretty, serene and not soothing, and dignified yet gladsome all the year, even in the stripped austerity of winter. It is probable that almost every traveller who has ever passed through Aix has been moved in some positive way by the view from one end of the Cours or the other, by the sounds of its fountains in the early hours, by the melodious play of the pure clear sunlight of Provence through its summer cave of leaves. . . . It is a man-made miracle, perhaps indescribable, compounded of stone and water and trees, and to the fortunate it is one of the world's chosen spots for their own sentient growth.

The trees and the fountains. At one end there is La Rotonde, a grandiose mid-nineteenth-century replacement for a more elegant confection dominated by Neptune with his sea horses; at the other, a statue of King René, *le bon Roi René*, holding a bunch of grapes. He deserves something more than a footnote, since it was he who presided over what came to be thought of as a golden age. He had been King of Naples until his expulsion by Alfonso of Aragon, but he was also Duc d'Anjou and Comte de Provence. He set up his court in Aix in 1442 and reigned there, benevolently and intelligently, for nearly forty years. He introduced the mulberry tree and the silkworm, and those muscat grapes which are commemorated in his statue. Life in Aix sounds idyliic, all roses and peacocks and courtly love, though it is no doubt sadly exaggerated. What is more historically true is the great rebuilding of the town during the seventeenth and eighteenth centuries. The fine houses still stand to give provenance; and it is not entirely by the way that one of the cardinal archbishops of Aix in the seventeenth century was called Mazarin, and was indeed the great statesman's brother.

But the fountains of Aix cannot be left without mention of the Fontaine des Quatre Dauphins. Here is Fisher again: "Its sound steals always down the four streets that stem out from it, and in summer generous chestnut trees bend toward it. Four of the merriest dolphins ever carved by man spout into the graceful basin under its stone needle, topped by a stone pine-cone, and it seems unlikely that anyone can pass by this exquisite whole without feeling reassured in some firm way."

A town of fountains and plane trees and fine houses, Aix. But one must not abandon it with the impression that Aix is a museum. It has its peculiar character as well as its problems. The posters and graffiti before the last French election displayed an unnerving enthusiasm for the far-right party. The immigrant problem spills over from Marseilles, and the streets of Aix have their quota of North Africans displaying leatherwork and cheap jewelry. On the other hand, Aix is also a university town, which introduces a political balance to right-wing excess, as well as a sense of liveliness and hope for the future.

The charm of Aix lies, of course, with its fountains and trees, and its fine buildings, converted into banks or *chocolatiers*. But it emanates also from its eccentricities: the exquisite Pavillon de Vendôme, built inevitably for a royal mistress and barely larger than a grand summer house; the appallingly maintained museums, most of them seemingly closed in perpetuity, and those that are open containing a mishmash of the truly awful intermingled with the occasional gem (if you like Ingres, there is a particularly repellent example of his work, "Jupiter and Thetis," in the Musée Granet, whose custodians were the only surly individuals I met in the whole of Aix); the old-fashioned haberdashers and the notices offering instructions in the *paso doble* (in French, shortened to *le paso*), the tango, and other somewhat passé dances.

And indeed dancing, dancing in the old style, flourishes in Aix. I once sat in a vast restaurant next door to the casino and watched the couples coming in on a wet and windy Saturday night, dressed to the nines, intent on dining well and expensively, and on dancing. The cheerful pianist would occasionally move over to a miniature electric organ, or pick up a musette accordion, thus giving the impression of an entire band in operation. Extremely old and nostalgic tunes like "Rose of Picardy" would alternate with popular Italian hits of the 1960s, and the diners would rise from their seats and execute the most phenomenal and intricate steps. It should have been comical, but it was endearing and rather impressive. It was a strange ritual—the dancers were welcomed affectionately by the maître d'hôtel and no doubt came every Saturday—but a charming one. They twirled and stamped and chasséed, and it was a serious business: no laughter, no false steps. It was Aix on a Saturday night, enjoying itself.

THERE COULD BE no greater contrast than that between Aix and Les Baux. When A. S. Forrest visited it at the turn of this century, he was immediately impressed by its air of desolation.

> The tall cypress-trees that in the plains spire up into the sky disappear as one ascends, and few shrubs or trees clothe the bald hillside. Wild thyme and lavender betray their presence by the fragrance of their perfume. Rabbits burrow amongst the undergrowth; hawks hover high overhead. Few other signs of life disturb the quiet of the lonely hills. From the crest of the chain, just before the descent into the great plains of La Crau, a weird scene breaks upon the eye. A valley of rocks, so fantastic, so unearthly, that one can easily credit the Provençal poet Mistral's belief that it was here that Dante got the inspiration for his graphic description of the topography of

the infernal regions. It is a valley of death, of ghosts, of skeletons, rocks naked and gaunt, altogether baffling description.

Les Baux is a ghost town. There are a couple of small hotels (the famous Baumanière is more agreeably positioned down in the valley), and there are the old bauxite quarries, there is the church of Saint Vincent, and there are the remains of the old castle, the "eagles' nest" which so exacerbated Richelieu that he ordered its destruction in 1632. Otherwise, there are only ghosts: of the troubadours and the Court of Love in the thirteenth century; of Guillaume de Cabestan, who was murdered by Raymond de Seillans, who suspected him of taking rather too direct an interest in Raymond's wife; of the unhappy woman herself, who, after being tricked into eating her dead admirer's heart nicely casseroled for dinner, went mad and threw herself onto the rocks below the castle; of *le bon Roi René,* whose influence on Provence was so considerable. Not far away is the mental home where Van Gogh lay after he cut off his ear; the de Sades lived in this part of Provence; and the iniquitous Raymond de Turenne enjoyed himself by watching his victims walk the plank into eternity over those bleak white rocks.

It is a sinister, depressing, oddly beautiful area, and a corrective to the usual picture of Provence as a sun-drenched earthly paradise. One should heed Elizabeth David's words: "Provence is not without its bleak and savage side. The inhabitants wage perpetual warfare against the ravages of the mistral; it takes a strong temperament to stand up to this ruthless wind which sweeps Provence for the greater part of the year. One winter and spring when the mistral never ceased its relentless screaming round our crumbling village opposite the Lubéron mountain we all seemed to come perilously near to losing our reason." Les Baux, too, is a place of madness and despair.

GREAT SEAPORTS are not like other cities. They are points of departure not nuclei of concentrated urban development. None more so than Marseilles. Jacques Ibert wrote a suite of musical picture postcards called *Escales,* and it would have been from Marseilles that his ship sailed, to the pleasure ports of Palermo and Tunis and Alexandria, above all to those stations on the map of French colonial power, the exotic sounds giving way to the hot and dusty reality: Brazzaville, Djibouti, Tananarive. The petty officials went out to tax and to govern, to civilize; the young girls, and those very nearly past marriageable age, went out to seek husbands and security, perhaps even love. It was not an organized migration but something more haphazard and hazardous. For the choice was so much thinner, the sphere of influence so much more restricted, the slow descent into boredom and unfaithfulness so much more predictable. And like an eternally self-repeating daguerreotype, more than a little foxed, back would come the daughters of those desiccated colonial couplings, searching for a scant education and a quick engagement.

As Richard Cobb says in *Promenades*, Marseilles must have presented an extraordinary picture of eager expectation and sad disillusionment:

> a general view of Marseilles, perched on the edge of its broken bowl, a huge amphitheatre open to seawards, must thus have marked, like the shutter of a camera, the departures and the arrivals of countless people, measuring out the regular course of a career in colonial service, with intervals of leave, new postings, gradual promotion, interrupted every now and then by alcoholisation or the regular return of malaria, marked too, possibly, by marriage, during one of those periods of leave, following the placing of a carefully worded advertisement—personal appearance, age, health, tastes, leisure habits, moral qualities, present employment, and future prospects specified—written out while in Abidjan or in Douala, in a specialised paper, such as *Le Chasseur Français,* the dream literature of the lonely colonial.

"The dream literature of the lonely colonial": a telling phrase which sums up the feelings of so many of the transients passing backward and forward through Marseilles. The last night before departure; the first night back. So many squalid little hotels, so many unsatisfactory brief encounters. "Even the gangling Bretonne or the massive Ardéchoise will represent the last physical link with *le pays,* so that *une passe,* in conditions however brief and breathless, takes on a much deeper significance, almost tender, maternal and lingering, long after physical contact has been broken." And, it must be remembered, Marseilles was once the *point de départ* for a huge colonial army. The streets around the

Hôtel de Ville and leading down to the Vieux Port would have seethed with soldiers desperate for a few final minutes of relief, of release from reality, perhaps even of a comforting arm. Marseilles exuded a heavy, heady perfume, the odor of sanctity mingled with the raw tang of the sexual act. Tomorrow we may die, but tonight we live.

The Zouaves and the Senegalese, above all the men from the Foreign Legion, hiding their pasts beneath their white képis, came and went, unremarked because, like cats, they were all the same in the dark. They were part of life and would perhaps soon be dead, of malaria, or a bullet, or an attack of accidie, but they would in any case be gone tomorrow, aboard one of the troopships bound for Equatorial Africa or Indochina or Madagascar.

> And so what a store then of metropolitan and transoceanic experience, of the minutiae of a social history well below the level of significant ambition—merely that humble one of *du galon,* an extra stripe, or a single one, or that, simpler still, to survive and to return—below that of any chronicled importance, even in an obscure regimental history, yet a wealth of human material stored, briefly at last, in the confused and crowded memory of tired street-walkers, as they relaxed, in couples or in threes, in a bar on the ground floor of their place of work, for a *menthe verte* or a *grenadine,* for a short respite to chat loudly with colleagues, between a series of *passes*—five minutes (*strictement chronométrées,* for profit is in speed)—gaudily dressed, frayed *dépôts d'archives humaines,* walking on abnormally high heels, each life not even afforded the tiny luxury of a Christian or even a nickname, not even identifiable in the simplest police terms, and so recollected, perhaps, in some exotic tattoo on the chest—because the customer would not even have had time to remove his shoes, much less to undress.

But France has lost her colonies, in the strictest sense, and the hotels with their neon signs and functional bedrooms are probably given over to traveling salesmen whose fears are for their jobs or their wives, in that order, rather than for an agonizing death at the hands of a Berber tribesman or the knife of a drunk French medical officer. The Vieux Port is given over to restaurants not to oceangoing liners or troopships. The disappearance of *la France*

d'outre-mer of the *colons* and the *pieds noirs* (French colonists of
Algeria), of the overseas colonial system, has rendered unnecessary
all the fixtures and fittings of a great port.

And yet, and yet . . . The gaudiness of Marseilles remains.
Not by the most crazed stretch of the imagination could it be
called a beautiful city. For a start, its architecture is almost wholly
nineteenth- and twentieth-century, and unless your taste runs to
the pompous or the vulgar it has little to offer. (Le Corbusier's
cité radieuse,* or *maison du fada* as it is known, is decried by the
Marseillais though it has a certain depressing fascination.) The
new cathedral is dreadful; the Musée des Beaux Arts possesses one
fine Tiepolo, a collection of superb and savage Daumiers, and a
great deal of rubbish; Louis XIV's Fort Saint Nicolas is impressive
but hardly exquisite; the Canebière, the English sailor's "can of
beer," is garish and interminable and packed.

It has its memories, of course. George Sand and Lamartine
and Prosper Mérimée all stayed at the Hôtel Beauvau at one time
or another. (George Sand loathed Marseilles because she was
snubbed by the locals who disapproved of her attachment to
Chopin and of her somewhat careless moral code in general.)
Rimbaud died in the Hôpital de la Conception. And Marcel Pagnol, with his plays and films and memoirs, established Marseilles
in the minds of countless people who would never alight at the
Gare Saint Charles or stroll along the Quai des Belges to find the
spot where King Alexander of Yugoslavia was assassinated. But it
is not, nor has it ever been, a place of culture or refinement. Marseilles, like many other seaports, has instead a reputation, often
exaggerated, but none the less potent. It is the reputation of a
wicked city, a place of pimps and prostitutes and cutthroats. In
1929, an American gentleman with the appealing name of Basil
Woon warned all tourists proposing to visit the South of France
to take special care:

> If you are interested in how the other side of the world lives,
> a trip through old Marseilles—by daylight—cannot fail to
> thrill, but it is not wise to venture into this district at night
> unless dressed like a stevedore and well armed. Thieves, cut-
> throats, and other undesirables throng the narrow alleys, and
> sisters of scarlet sit in the doorways of their places of business,

* *Literally "radiant city." It is a matter of taste.*

catching you by the sleeve as you pass by. The dregs of the world are here, unsifted. It is Port Said, Shanghai, Barcelona, and Sydney combined. Now that San Francisco has reformed, Marseilles is the world's wickedest port.

This is good stirring stuff. One expects to see Jean Gabin, cigarette jutting, revolver at the ready, leaning against a wall; a chorus line of whores waiting to pounce; Pagnol's lovable fishermen and tarts gone suddenly sour and menacing. But one man's view is no more reliable than any other's. Compare all this with Mme de Sévigné, writing in more elegant times: "I am ecstatic about the peculiar beauty of this town. Yesterday, the weather was heavenly and the place where I looked over the sea, the fortresses, the mountains, and the city is astonishing. . . . I must apologise to Aix, but Marseilles is lovelier and livelier than it, in proportion to Paris itself! There are at least a hundred thousand people here; and I cannot even try to count how many of them are beauties: the whole atmosphere makes me somewhat untrustworthy!" A far cry from the soap factories and the olive oil distilleries, the crush on the Canebière.

Mme de Sévigné was writing in 1672, and no doubt she paid little attention to the Château d'If, that sinister memorial to the savagery of earlier days perched on its limestone island. Here is the real menace of Marseilles: the sailor confined to a black, stinking, windowless cell for striking an officer, and who survived, blind, deaf, and mad, for thirty years; the innumerable Huguenot prisoners on their way to the galleys at Toulon; the Man in the Iron Mask incarcerated here before his removal to the Bastille for some threat to the King or the state which has never been revealed; even, fictionally, Dumas's Count of Monte Cristo.

As the motorboat takes its passengers back to the Quai des Belges from the prison island, Marseilles looks much as it did a hundred years ago: "the two forts at each side of the mouth of the old harbour, the mosque-like contours of the cathedral, a place apparently of Eastern worship and rite, the huge Virgin at the summit of Endoum, the beige, russet and mauve hills." But this is deceptive. The *pont transbordeur* has gone from the old harbor, only the yachts and the *balancelles* which transport oranges from the Balearics ride at anchor; the maze of narrow, dirty streets which was the Quartier du Vieux Port was blown up by the Germans in 1943 and replaced after the liberation by exceedingly ugly blocks of flats. Marseilles has lost its raison d'être. It is no longer a *lieu de passage,* a stepping-off point . . . to what? Richard Cobb describes it as "a sort of twilight zone in careers spent in the colonies or in the colonial armies: a threshold, neither one thing nor another, neither quite the *métropole,* nor quite the African or Far Eastern shore, but suspended in a point of time and space between the two, and so a time and place for uncomfortable self-examination, doubt, bewilderment, hope, and fear. Of such passers-through," he concludes, "there is no visible record."

What is left? Surely something more than the *galéjade,* or tall story, celebrated by Marcel Pagnol's characters; the mutual contempt which lingers between Paris and Marseilles, the brash vibrancy of the Canebière? Perhaps M. F. K. Fisher comes closest to the spirit of the place:

> Meanwhile, Marseilles lives, with a unique strength that plainly scares less virile breeds. Its people are proud of being "apart," and critics mock them for trying to sound even more Italianate than they are, trying to play roles for the tourists. . . . The Pinball Boys are thinner and more viperous there than anywhere in Europe . . . and the tarts are tarter and the old hags older and more haggish than anywhere in the world. Behind this almost infantile enjoyment of playing their parts on a superb stage with changing backdrops that are certainly *insolite,* and a full orchestration of every sound-effect from the ringings of great bells to the whine of the tramontane and the vicious howl of the mistral, held together by sirens from ambulances and ships, and the pinpricks of complaining seagulls . . . behind this endlessly entertaining and absorbing melodrama, a secret life-source provides its inner nourishment to the citizens.

Reality has superseded artifice. All Marseilles is a stage.

STENDHAL THOUGHT Marseilles the prettiest town in France (in his opinion, Bordeaux was the most beautiful). He was less complimentary about Cannes. When he visited it in May 1838, he admired "the charming white villas surrounded by tall olive trees and oak groves" but noted a formidable deterrent to anyone intending to settle there.

A Monsieur Dumas has been obliged to have the ancient elms that shade his château cut down. He had been told this would let in more air and would prevent fever. Unhealthy stagnant waters, far from there and much lower down behind the point of land that juts out toward the island of Sainte-Marguerite on the Golfe Juan which has become so famous, have poisoned this whole mountain. In times past, half of Cannes suffered from fever in the month of August. At last it occurred to the authorities to clean up a little river that flows to the east of Cannes, and the fever disappeared. All the same, household waters and the three cesspools of Cannes poison the pretty promenade along the sea.

Nothing changes.

Four years before Stendhal's visit, Cannes was nothing more than a small fishing village. Lord Brougham, the former Lord Chancellor and once champion of Queen Caroline during her extremely public quarrel with George IV, was on his way to Italy with his sick daughter. He got no further than Cannes. The authorities had closed the frontier because of a cholera epidemic in France, so Lord Brougham and his daughter put up at the only hotel in the town. He fell in love with the place and decided to build a villa on the road to Fréjus. His daughter died, but he continued to spend the winters there for the next thirty-four years. He also persuaded Louis-Philippe to provide the money for the building of a harbor, so that the perfumes of Grasse, up in the hills behind Cannes, need no longer be taken the long route to Marseilles.

Brougham's example was soon imitated by other Englishmen. Villas sprang up, the railway line was extended to Cannes in 1863, and regattas in the harbor began in 1860. The Prince of Wales, almost inevitably, came in 1872 to play baccarat and to stay at the new Gray d'Albion Hotel. The foundation stone of the casino was laid by the Grand Duke Michael in 1906, and the vast Carlton Hotel followed six years later.

William Scott wrote a book about the French and Italian Rivieras in 1907. He commented rather stuffily on Cannes.

In comparing the principal towns of the Côte d'Azur a French writer has said that "Cannes est le pays où l'on jouit de la vie" [the place where one enjoys life]. The judgment is a just one, for here the climate, the position, the surroundings, the associations, all unite to favour the place as a winter resort; and to render it less dependent on amusements, excitements, or indulgence of various kinds. Life can be enjoyed and be pleasant enough without them, if personal worry, that arch enemy, be absent. This characteristic is reflected in the place itself, in the habits, and in the composition of the foreign colony. There is a certain indefinable selectness, superiority if you will, or perhaps one should say distinction, to be noted in looking around. It is not less cosmopolitan than its rivals, but there is less of the "rowdy" element than in some places, and less of the mere invalid element than in others. Wealthy and leisured people come here to be quiet, to pass the winter in favourable surroundings, and while not disdaining pleasure are not given to undue excitement. Opinions are divided [and here Mr. Scott veers toward the tendentious] as to whether the recently erected Municipal Casino is going to be a blessing or the reverse. Cannes has at last decided to bring herself more nearly into line with some of her rivals, and to provide certain desirable opportunities for legitimate entertainment which have hitherto been lacking. If proper care be exercised in directing the enterprise, it need not necessarily lead to an influx of those rowdy and undesirable elements from which this most select of winter resorts has hitherto been free; but the task before its managers is not an easy one, and the temptations to err on the side of too great laxity are very considerable.

Well, not necessarily. After all, as Mr. Scott reminded his readers, "in 1887 her late Majesty our beloved Queen Victoria passed some time in the Villa Edelweiss," and a memorial church and fountain had recently been erected in memory of her son the Duke of Albany, who died in Cannes in 1884. Surely the proprieties would be maintained, people would behave with decorum, the "rowdy and undesirable elements" would be kept at bay, Cannes would remain sacrosanct to the rich, the gentlemanly, above all to the English.

As Mr. Scott should have been well aware, the minute a resort was taken up and patronized by Edward, Prince of Wales, vulgarity and license were bound to break out. Sexual mores would go by the board, gambling for high stakes would occupy the evenings, and as for the nights . . . Another Babylon had been born.

In the 1920s, the South of France, and Cannes in particular, became what many a journalist termed "the playground of Europe." The old fashion of merely wintering on the Riviera had passed into oblivion. Now anyone who was anyone, and large quantities of people who wished to become someone, flocked southward to expose their white skins to the fierce Mediterranean sun. The need to maintain at all costs a pure, delicate complexion by concealing oneself under a whole battery of hats and parasols was replaced by a passion for brown skins, and the browner the better. A suntan was thought sexy (though the word would not have been used), above all it denoted that the bearer could afford to go to the South of France. The elements became distinctly rowdy; laxity was rife.

Our old friend William Scott could see it all happening back in 1907. In a chapter entitled "Some People One Meets" (and one can almost sense the shudder of disgust), he paints a picture in the gaudiest of colors:

> It is a motley and cosmopolitan crowd that gathers yearly on the shores of the Mediterranean, and fills the streets of its chief winter cities. The wealth, the beauty, the leaders, and the idlers of the Old World and the New jostle each other, sometimes literally and not too lightly, under the blue skies, on the broad promenades, and in the gambling-rooms of the Riviera. We meet priests, pedants, and politicians, royalties and rowdies, misery and madness, gamblers and gourmands, as well as frumps and flirts of varying ages and conditions. Around us are sportsmen and speculators, spies and swindlers, the splendid strength of athletic manhood, the masterful energy of superb intellect, the fairest flowers of a pure and noble womanhood, the shamefullest grades of a painted and bespangled degradation. The gayest, proudest, richest portion of this mass of fluttering humanity swarms on the French Riviera, the Côte d'Azur, flaunts its butterfly wings in the sunshine, or scorches them at its glaring gas-jets.

If poor Mr. Scott could have been transported in a time machine to the beaches of Cannes during the Film Festival, perhaps at the height of the Bardot Era in the 1960s with all its attendant nudity (nothing compared with the 1980s) and general shenanigans, he would have seen plenty of bespangled degradation, though superb intellect and pure noble womanhood might have been in short supply. What Queen Victoria might have thought beggars the imagination.

THE QUEEN EMPRESS would certainly not have been amused by Saint-Tropez, which Brigitte Bardot did so much to popularize. Mr. Scott ignores it entirely, for the very good reason that it is a recent phenomenon. Recent as a phenomenon it may be, but its historical roots run deep. The dispute over the origin of its name gives some indication of how old the town is. Some say that the name stems from Torpes, who was one of Nero's officers, a Christian, and who was martyred at Pisa. His body was, for no accountable reason, placed in a boat together with a dog and a cock and sent on its way (the head remained in Pisa). After nineteen days, the boat beached on the south coast of France, and Saint-Tropez was born. The second version is slightly more credible: Saint-Tropez is a corruption of *san trovato,* the found saint, after a ship's figurehead washed up and venerated by fishermen. The third is merely amusing, involving as it does the unearthing of a statue of Hermes, whose impressive sexual organs had to be demolished before it could be allowed as a Christian patron saint.

Saint-Tropez went through the usual run of disasters and reconstructions during the Dark and Middle Ages (both the Moors and Good King René crop up), and its ships helped beat off a small Spanish armada in 1637. The most famous Saint-Tropézien was the Bailli de Suffren, the dashing admiral who caused a considerable amount of nuisance to the British during the American War of Independence; his greenish statue stands in front of a hotel on the waterfront and looks both martial and slightly comic.

But it is as a colony of artists and writers that Saint-Tropez became known. Guy de Maupassant and, much later, Colette came; and a whole range of Neo-Impressionist painters recorded various scenes of the town and the harbor. In the Musée de l'Annonciade, one of the most delightful galleries in the world, there are pictures by Signac and Seurat, Matisse and Bonnard, Derain and Vuillard, Dufy and Dunoyer de Segonzac, a remarkable collection of truly happy and enlivening paintings.

Nowadays there are really two Saint-Tropezes, and they need to be differentiated. There is the raffish, moneyed, rather vulgar

Saint-Tropez, which concentrates down by the sleek yachts in the harbor, moves from hotel to restaurant to nightclub to swimming pool, wears the most extraordinary fashions, and is there basically to be seen, admired, and even condemned. In season, the Quai de Suffren, and in particular the favorite café, Sénéquier, is like a twentieth-century "Tentation de Saint-Antoine." The clothes are preposterous, the hair is dyed, the faces are lifted, the scent of money and sex is in the air. The silver candelabra are lit on the yachts and the white-bumfreezered stewards pour the champagne. The common herd peers and pries and ogles, and feasts pruriently on the fantasy world laid out before it. It is all incredibly self-regarding, and public, and strangely innocent, like a stage set on which the participants only simulate an orgy of pleasure to the point of satiation.

But in the comparative cool of the morning, and at all times once the fashionable crowds have departed at the end of the summer, the real Saint-Tropez re-emerges. In the Place des Lices, the old men play boules and sit drinking a pastis or a beer outside the Café des Artistes. Up the steep streets above the harbor, near the cathedral, in the little plane-shaded squares, people go shopping for everyday necessities; the day's catch lies invitingly in the minuscule fish market; even down on the Quai de Suffren you can sit on one of Sénéquier's maroon-colored chairs and sip an espresso coffee without feeling that you are in a fish tank along with those crustaceans awaiting tonight's depredations. With the sunlight shining on the freshly watered pavements, the yachts departed for Cannes or Antibes or Monte Carlo, the sound of the cathedral's bells in the air, and the old ladies in their black dresses going about their business, Saint-Tropez has been given back to the Saint-Tropéziens. If only Saint-Tropez were not a cul-de-sac, one feels, at the end of a promontory which goes nowhere, perhaps it would be different, private and peaceful like its near neighbors, Ramatuelle and Gassin. But then it would no longer be a phenomenon.

Is MONTE CARLO French? Yes and no. It is not quite the end of the line. The train still has to run through Menton—Mentone, as it was always called when English maiden ladies went there for the winter—before it reaches the frontier at Ventimiglia and descends toward Genoa. Perhaps it is a figment of the imagination, neither French, nor Italian, nor even Monégasque. Certainly, it has no place with the realities of life. It is as artificial as Toytown, as cloying as the marzipan on a wedding cake; it belongs in a Cole Porter lyric, or a Noel Coward sketch, or a Somerset Maugham short story. It is fun.

Strange things happen in Monte Carlo. Gamblers shoot themselves. Sometimes they even win. Here is Graham Greene setting the scene in *Loser Takes All:* "I put on my dressing-gown and went out on to my balcony. The front of the Casino was floodlit: it looked like a cross between a Balkan palace and a super-cinema with the absurd statuary sitting on the edge of the green roof looking down at the big portico and the commissionaires; everything stuck out in the white light as though projected in 3D. In the harbour the yachts were all lit up, and a rocket burst in the air over the hill of Monaco. It was so stupidly romantic I could have wept."

He loses, and then he wins, massively, to the tune of 5 million francs. And Monte Carlo is waiting for people who are winners. "One adapts oneself to money much more easily than to poverty; Rousseau might have written that man was born rich and is everywhere impoverished. It gave me great satisfaction to pay back the manager and leave my key at the desk. I frequently rang the bell for the pleasure of confronting a uniform without shame. . . . I ordered the Gruaud-Larose 1934 (I even sent it back because it was not the right temperature). I had our things moved to a suite and I hired a car to take us to the beach. At the beach I hired one of the private bungalows where we could sunbathe, cut off by bushes and shrubs from the eyes of common people." For there is no place for common people in Monte Carlo.

Monte Carlo has always evoked envy and disapproval in equal measure. William Scott remarked on this in 1907: "So great has been the prejudice against Monte Carlo in certain quarters that even the late Bishop of Gibraltar for a long time conscientiously hesitated to sanction the establishing of a church and clergyman in the neighbourhood, although one would have thought—if the estimate of its morality or immorality were correct—it was precisely in such a situation that Church work could be most usefully undertaken." It is possible, of course, that the worthy bishop foresaw the involvement of the Papacy with the Monte Carlo casino as leading shareholders. Scott was, however, censorious of some of the habits practiced by the management of the casino. He was scandalized to discover that Lord Salisbury, a former Prime Minister no less, had been turned away because he was unsuitably dressed; so too had—though not simultaneously—the celebrated actress Ellen Terry and a bishop of Mr. Scott's acquaintance (perhaps the Bishop of Gibraltar seeking further and better particulars); and an English duke, because he had had the temerity or bad taste to wear trousers with turn-ups, had unceremoniously been shown the door.

Scott's knowledge of the casino at Monte Carlo is impressive, and a trifle worrying. He tells the story of a particularly pious Scottish Presbyterian minister taking his family to the casino in order to demonstrate the extreme sinfulness of gambling and being converted on the spot by a particularly exciting run on red. And there was the man who spent half the time distributing religious tracts while informing anyone who cared to listen that he had "found peace in Jesus," and the rest gambling his and his wife's money away as fast as the roulette wheel could turn. But he rallies with a fine denunciation of his own:

> There is, of course, a sad dark side to all this glare of light, fury of wild excitement, splendour of costly costumes, and beauty of lovely flowers. The strains of perfect music do but drown the shrieks of wild despair, and the blaze of a million gas-jets can never break up the darkness that settles down on many a blasted life, ruined home, or perished honour. . . . There are few of us who have lived long in this fascinating neighbourhood yet have not known some friend come to utter grief through having yielded to the fatal passion, having been unable to stay his hand from the folly which would blight his future life. Fewer still have not seen or known cases so sad that the very memory of them calls up a feeling of acute pain. Even when life is left to the victim, how often has reason taken its departure; and now the poor useless brain throbs ever to the fancied whirl of the roulette wheel, or the fleeting chances of the "rouge et noir."

One should perhaps reveal that the Monte Carlo casino (not to be confused with the Summer Sporting Club, which is by the sea) was built by Charles Garnier, who was also the architect of the Paris Opéra; and one should not forget that Diaghilev's ballet company had its headquarters there, and that many French composers were commissioned to write operas which were first performed at Monte Carlo (the best was Ravel's *L'Enfant et les Sortilèges* to a text by Colette, which had its première in 1925). Nor should one ignore the other pleasures of the tiny principality of Monaco. It has a pretty pink palace, a fine aquarium, a grand harbor where the yachts of Onassis and Niarchos and other millionaires once lay, an army of twenty-four chocolate soldiers, a rally and a grand prix motor race, and a reigning family, the Grimaldis, whose current head, Prince Rainier, once had the good taste to marry the beautiful Philadelphian Grace Kelly. All would indeed seem to be *luxe, calme et volupté.*

But there is, of course, a dark side to Monte Carlo besides the occasional suicide or bankrupt. I know of a curious case which occurred some twenty-five years ago. I imagine the participants are all dead, but I will disguise the names even so.

Monte Carlo has always been something of a mecca for rich widows. The poor ones used to go to Bordighera; now they reside in London's South Kensington. There was one in particular, a rich American lady (there are no poor American widows) who had married an officer in a Highland regiment. Mrs. Mackenzie—let us call her that—had lived for many years, comfortably though never extravagantly, in a well-run hotel of the second rank, not in the least flashy or luxurious, somewhere to the west of the casino. It had a good British name: Was it the Buckingham, or the Montrose, or the Devonshire? Something like that, though not precisely.

Mrs. Mackenzie had no children, but her husband had been a distant cousin of my paternal grandfather's. I did not often go to Monte Carlo, but I was as a very young man somewhat intoxicated by its glamour, and did find myself there on a few occasions. I visited Mrs. Mackenzie at her discreet hotel, and we lunched or dined in the restaurant there on impeccably English food of the old-fashioned variety. Roast beef followed by bread-and-butter pudding, and preceded by clear soup and a white fish of dubious ancestry, is not my idea of an ideal menu for a hot summer's day, but it was no doubt all very wholesome and easily digested. There was always, perhaps in deference to Mrs. Mackenzie's American blood, a cocktail before the meal. And afterwards there might be a visit to the casino. She never won or lost more than five pounds. It was a ritual, not a habit.

As I have said, Mrs. Mackenzie had no children; indeed I was possibly the closest relation she had. We got on well; I became very fond of her; we corresponded in a desultory, undemanding way.

Then the letters from Monte Carlo ceased. Instead, I received a letter from a well-known firm of London solicitors. Rather to my surprise, I was told that I was the main beneficiary under Mrs. Mackenzie's will, though no sum was specified. Could I help locate her, however? Had I heard from her recently? I replied that I had not, but offered to write to the hotel manager. Some months passed, and then a letter with a Monaco postmark appeared one morning. The manager regretted *infiniment* to inform me that Madame Mackenzie had died. She had, apparently, been suffering from senile dementia—hence the lack of response to my and the solicitors' letters—and had been removed to her doctor's private clinic. She had not survived the move more than a few months.

There was, of course, a new will, witnessed by two servants in the hotel. The chief beneficiaries were . . . Yes, almost too neatly, the hotel manager and the doctor. One cannot help surmising.

ONE SHOULD NOT leave the South of France on a sour note. It is still one of the most spectacularly beautiful parts of Europe. The smell of the pine trees and the wild thyme still intoxicates. The oleanders and Provence roses still bloom. The sea sparkles. Inland, the earth bakes; the grapes and figs ripen. To quote Alan Houghton Brodrick: "There is nothing trivial or terrifying. It is all very Mediterranean and reasonable . . ."

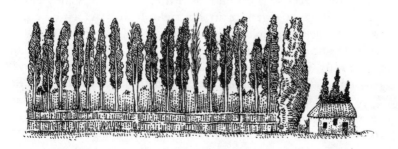

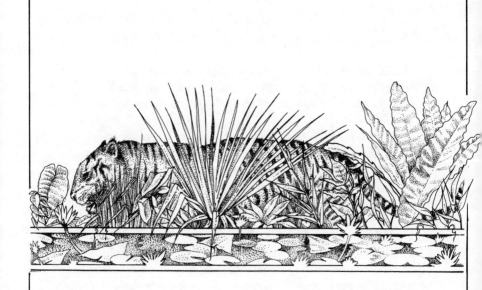

x

Outre-Mer, Overseas

*I*N LE DOUANIER ROUSSEAU's famous portrait of Pierre Loti, naval officer, writer, and eccentric, the latter stands gazing out at us, a cigarette in his right hand, factory chimneys and belching smoke over his right shoulder, and a small cat with elegant ringed markings and a mildly startled expression sitting firmly in the foreground. On Loti's head—and evidently painted in after the hair—is a red fez or *chéchia*, as worn by the Zouaves or Spahis. It is a perfect touch of the exotic superimposed on what is already an unusual portrait of a traveler and adventurer painted by a man obsessed with outlandish images: lions lurking in jungles, gorillas fighting with Indians, huge brightly colored tropical flowers. And in Rousseau's most celebrated painting, the "Snake Charmer," of 1907, all the elements of the exotic seem to fuse. A mysterious dark figure stands on the edge of a dense tropical forest beside a river playing a flute. Snakes rear up from the undergrowth or hang entranced from the trees. A pretty pink bird with a splayed bill looks on admiringly. The moon, full and yellow, shines overhead. It is impossible, and unnecessary, to analyze exactly what is going on in the picture. Michel Hoog says of it: "At that period of exploration, of colonial expeditions, and of the intensive development of religious missions, the image of the savage whom people wish to 'civilise' but who retains an 'innocence' which evokes a certain nostalgia remains ambiguous, as it is in this painting, or in those pictures of his exact contemporary, Gauguin, to whom he is so close. The fauna in Gauguin's South Seas paintings (horses, dogs, pigs, peacocks) is, it is true, a domesticated fauna, but with Gauguin as with the 'Snake Charmer' the figure deep in the equatorial flora has a significance which is more incantatory than anecdotal."

Three years earlier, Jane Bathori had given the first performance of Ravel's song cycle *Shéhérazade,* with Alfred Cortot conducting. These were settings of three poems by Tristan Klingsor, "Asie," "La Flute Enchantée," and "L'Indifférent," all of them undeniably exotic, as Klingsor himself acknowledged: "The Orient was in the air: through Bakst, Rimsky and Dr. Mardrus, who translated *The Thousand and One Nights.* The symbolists had transposed their feelings by presenting them through a veil of legendary fiction. I thought of presenting mine through a Persian veil. A Persia of fantasy, of course." The first song, "Asie," is full of enticing, languorous images perfectly realized by Ravel's music. We are in a world of cadis and viziers, opium pipes and turbans, minarets and schooners with violet sails, Chinese mandarins and beautiful princesses. And with the exotic goes cruelty, just as in James Elroy Flecker's *Hassan.* The final verse exudes a slightly sickly mixture of beauty and brutality:

> *I should like to see assassins smiling*
> *at the executioner who cuts off an innocent head*
> *With his great curved oriental sword;*
> *I should like to see poor people and queens;*
> *I should like to see roses and blood;*

I should like to see people dying of love or of hatred,
and then return home later
to tell my story to those who are interested in dreams,
raising, like Sinbad,
my old Arabian cup
from time to time up to my lips,
in order to interrupt the tale artfully.

Klingsor mentions Bakst and the Russian composers, but the French involvement with the exotic ran far deeper. The basis was, not surprisingly, two-tiered: colonial and parochial. France was at the center of a great colonial empire almost as far-flung as the British Empire. And in one way it was far more complex. The British had wrested Canada from the French (the Indians were rather forgotten), and Australia and New Zealand from the Aborigines and Maoris respectively. But the natives—to use what has become a derogatory term—were thought of as savages with no culture, above all with no civilization in the broadest sense. Therefore these vast empty spaces were easily colonized and assimilated, and the British white way of life was easily developed.

The French spheres of influence were generally in parts of the world where there was a long local tradition of culture, very often stretching back far beyond the flowering of French civilization. The Near East (particularly Syria), North Africa, Indochina, Polynesia, China—these were the areas which provided the spots of color on France's imperial global map. This is an exaggeration, of course, since the argument takes no account of Guiana or the French West Indies or New Caledonia or French Equatorial Africa, whose eminently recognizable and admirable cultures would not have been recognized, let alone admired, in the nineteenth century. But the point has nevertheless some foundation. And what it meant was that people of "exotic" aspect and culture were seen even in Paris. The French colonial army, too, was recruited far more regularly from local troops than was ever the case, could ever be the case, with Britain (India being the exception). Canadians, Australians, New Zealanders, even South Africans, would all rally to Britain's call to arms in 1914 and 1939, but these were white, mainly Anglo-Saxon troops, indeed, dare one say it, to all intents and purposes British. The Zouaves and Spahis and all the other brilliantly accoutered French colonial regiments were brown or black or yellow, but they fought for France and were a perfectly normal sight on the boulevards of Paris or along the harbor of Marseilles in peacetime, and in the trenches on the Western Front during the First World War.

So, for European France, there was a constant taste of the exotic. But that was too thin a diet for some. Pierre Loti played on the taste, Daudet thought it worth satirizing, countless poets gave themselves up to it, and in a later generation novelists like Camus and Malraux were obsessed by it. But it is through the music and art of France that it can be most easily looked at.

In music and painting, just as in literature, there were inevitably always opposing forces and opinions. Nothing could be less exotic than the landscapes of the Barbizon school, or indeed of the majority of the great Impressionists; for them, the forest of Fontainebleau, Monet's garden at Giverny, the banks of the Seine, the streets of Paris, the flashy silks of the jockeys at Longchamps or the dancers at the barre were the subjects. (Even Toulouse-Lautrec's touches of realism are no more exotic than a novel of Zola's.) Paul Gauguin represents the other side, the deep fascination for *outre-mer,* for overseas, and he does so with virtuosic passion.

He had decided to give up his comfortable, successful bourgeois existence at the age of thirty-four in 1883 and paint (the stifling conformity of Paris was always likely to produce the occasional thunderclap). As if that break with the past were not enough, eight years later he decided to abandon his family and his country and go to Tahiti. It was one of the most extraordinary, and extraordinarily influential, decisions in the history of art. In *Noa Noa,* he recorded his impressions of this utterly new world: "For sixty-three days I have been on my way, and I burn to reach the longed-for land. On June 8 we saw strange fires moving about in zig-zags—fishermen. Against a dark sky a jagged black cone stood out. We were rounding Moorea and coming in sight of Tahiti."

The old King was dying, and the Tahitians were visibly affected. "In the roadstead an unusual stir of boats with orange sails, upon the blue sea frequently crossed by the silvered ripples from the line of the reefs. The inhabitants of the neighbouring islands were coming in, each day, to be present at their king's last moment, at the final taking-over of their islands by the French." But it was the funeral which opened Gauguin's eyes. It began badly. The monument set up in King Pomaré's memory was appalling, coral lumps held together with cement. The French Governor La-

cascade (a name surely invented by Feydeau) made a speech—
"usual cliché"—which was duly translated. The Protestant pastor
made a speech. The Queen's brother made a speech. And that was
all. Except that, on the way back—"as though returning from the
races"—everyone's spirits miraculously lifted.

> All these people, so grave during the last few days, began
> laughing again; *vahines* [Tahitian men] once more took their
> *tanes* [Tahitian women] by the arm, wagging their buttocks,
> while their broad bare feet ponderously trampled the dust of
> the roadway. Arrived near the Fatana river, a general scat-
> tering. In some places, women, hiding among the stones,
> crouched in the water with their skirts raised to the girdle,
> cleansing their thighs of the soiling dust from the road, cool-
> ing their knees which the march and the heat had chafed.
> Thus restored they again took the road for Papeete, their
> breasts leading and the conical shells which tipped their nip-
> ples drawing the muslin of their dresses to a point, with all
> the suppleness and grace of a healthy animal, and spreading
> round about them that mixture of animal scent and sandal-
> wood and gardenias. *"Teine merahi Noa Noa* (how very fra-
> grant)," they said.

"Animal scent and sandalwood and gardenias," a heady mixture indeed. And Gauguin, saddened by this final act in the history
of an old civilization, began to paint. He painted, obsessively, for
two years. His journal is full of colors—blue and orange, silver and
black, gold and green—and his paintings seem to vibrate, to come
at you. Two of the finest are "Vahine no te Tiare" ("Woman with
a Flower") of 1891 and "Nafea Faa Ipoipo?" ("When Will You
Marry?") painted the following year. In the first, the marvelously
serene face seems to be concealing inner contemplation. The woman
wears a purple dress, she holds an orange flower in her right hand,
her hair is a deep black, she is posed against a red background, and
there are touches of bright green here and there. The second painting is all scarlet and emerald and corn-yellow and deep blue. The
exotic and the real are fused.

One wonders whether Gauguin should ever have returned to
Paris. It was, in a way, an admission of failure, at best a half-term
report. His 1893 exhibition was certainly a failure, though Gauguin tried to persuade himself otherwise. The critics used words
like "brutal," "coarse," and "revolting." One wrote of "the fanta-

sies of a poor cracked mind," and the playwright Strindberg confessed himself baffled: "I cannot understand your art and cannot like it. I have no grasp of your art, which is now exclusively Tahitian." Gauguin himself realized the special nature of his art. He once called himself a "savage-in-spite-of-myself." And Nicholas Wadley puts his finger on the truth when he describes Gauguin as "a civilized man with a vision of an ideal, primitive existence—a blending of dream and reality."

Gauguin returned to Tahiti in 1895, and went on to the Marquesas Islands six years later. He died in 1903. To the end, he retained his inimitable attitude toward life and art. "The French thought of him as savage and the natives thought of him as French." He was not unhappy.

IT WOULD BE difficult to think of anyone less like Gauguin than Maurice Ravel, and yet he too personifies that lust for the exotic which runs in the veins of so many Frenchmen. Photographs of him show an elegant, rather world-weary face, cigarette hanging, the face of a typical flâneur, a well-dressed, well-heeled boulevardier. He had a passion for cocktails, he liked jazz, he enjoyed high society. Unlike Debussy and Chausson, he was not greatly influenced by the music of Wagner. But a list of the composers who taught or influenced him is interesting: Fauré, Chabrier, and Satie. The first provided the fastidious classicism which would later be expressed in works like *Le Tombeau de Couperin,* the *Pavane for a Dead Infanta* and the *Introduction and Allegro.* Chabrier, whose *España* was immensely popular, reinforced Ravel's own background (he was born in the Basque village of Ciboure) and inspired the opera *L'Heure Espagnole,* the *Spanish Rhapsody,* and the *Alborada del Gracioso.* And Satie provided the wit and the eccentricity. (Few pieces of music are more eccentric than Ravel's *Boléro,* with its motif endlessly repeated toward a final crescendo; few wittier than some of Ravel's songs or the parodies in the exquisite opera *L'Enfant et les Sortilèges.*)

But there is yet another facet of Ravel's music. In his lovely ballet *Ma Mère l'Oye,* inspired by Perrault's fairy stories, there is one dazzling episode entitled "Laideronnette, Impératrice des Pagodes." A perfect Oriental atmosphere, slightly reminiscent of the gamelan music of Indonesia, delicate and tinkling, is created. There is something rather similar in the *Piano Concerto for the Left*

Hand. In the second movement of the *Piano Trio*, which Ravel called "Pantoum," there are further exotic sounds. And the *Chansons Madécasses* (*Madagascar*) speak for themselves. *Tzigane* gives us Hungary; *La Valse*, Vienna; one of the greatest ballet scores ever composed, *Daphnis and Chloé*, classical Greece; the "Blues" movement in the *Violin Sonata*, the opening movement of the *Piano Concerto*, and the foxtrot in *L'Enfant et les Sortilèges*, the United States. The world—east, west, south (but never north, there is nothing exotic about the north)—is laid out before us.

No other French composer quite achieves this sense of the exotic, of which *Shéhérazade* was the most obvious product. Darius Milhaud was influenced by the music of Brazil and of America; Debussy occasionally conjured up the heat of Spain; Satie composed some cool evocations of classical Greece; the exoticism of Saint-Saëns or Delibes or Massenet was pretty but essentially ersatz; Poulenc, mentally, barely abandoned the chic of Paris, let alone the frontiers of France. But even Ravel's *Boléro*, greatly decried by the critics, retains its popularity because it is, first and foremost, exotic. It, too, belongs to *outre-mer*.

LE DOUANIER ROUSSEAU is perhaps the Satie rather than the Ravel of French painting, and in his pictures the naive and the exotic are perfectly blended. Like Gauguin, he delighted in primary colors, orange, red, sky-blue, green, to which he would add shocking pink and purple and silvery white. One of his most mysterious paintings is the "Bohémienne Endormie," which he painted in 1897 and which now hangs in New York's Museum of Modern Art. Rousseau described the subject matter in a letter to the Mayor of Laval, whom he hoped to persuade to buy the canvas: "A wandering negress, a player on the mandolin, with a jar beside her (a pitcher containing drinking water) is in a deep sleep worn out by fatigue. A lion happens to be passing, sniffs her, does not devour her. It is an effect of the moonlight, very poetic. The scene takes place in a completely arid desert. The gipsy woman is wearing oriental clothes." It is hardly surprising that the Mayor of Laval was not won over by this amazing description. The picture sounds preposterous, and in many ways it is preposterous. But it is mesmeric, irresistible. The woman has very large feet, but wears an exceedingly elegant dress, striped like a deck chair, every color of the rainbow; her mattress is similarly striped; the mandolin belongs to Picasso. No wonder the lion did not proceed to make a meal of her. He looks, in any case, like an amiable toy, with his mane swept up and one very glittering eye inspecting this strange phenomenon lying in the middle of the desert. Cocteau thought it surreal, which it is, but also anticipating the Cubists, which is doubtful. What it is, without doubt, is exotic. Alas, the Mayor of Laval was not much taken with exotica. He might have preferred one of Rousseau's paintings of dirigibles or airplanes, though they, too, offer images which are hardly commonplace.

It can, of course, be argued that simply because Gauguin and Rousseau were not understood, let alone appreciated, during their lifetimes, the innate French interest in *outre-mer* is at best an occasional eccentricity and at worst a myth. Certainly the riot which surrounded the first performance in Paris of Stravinsky's *Rite of Spring* would not have led one to believe that the audience was full of devotees of the exotic. (The riposte would no doubt have been that the music was barbaric and crude rather than exotic, which has softer, more pleasing connotations.) But, often in spite of themselves, the French have never been able to avoid the confrontation between French normality and the magnetic attraction of overseas, whether it was a hot, dusty, unhealthy colonial outpost in the Ivory Coast or Senegal or French Guiana, or whether it was the cosmopolitan joie de vivre of Algiers or Saigon.

Colonies provide pleasures and problems, the latter usually predominating. Gauguin's Tahiti or Camus's Algeria or Malraux's Indochina are fixed forever as emanations of, and in a way celebrations of, the French Empire. Uproar in New Caledonia or Guadaloupe still hits the headlines. Revolution in Réunion could still bring down a government. The sins of the fathers are always with us. At least, though, writers, artists, and musicians have been inspired by, and have repaid their debt to, what the colonial adventurers originally carved out for profit and French aggrandizement.

xi

La Gloire

IF YOU STAND in the courtyard in front of the Palace of Versailles, or in the center of the Place des Victoires in Paris, and look up, you will see the personification of *la gloire française*. There, on what in historical novels of the old school is termed a mettlesome steed, is Louis XIV, indeed in all his glory. Arrogance, power, self-confidence, a passionate disregard for the pettiness of life, all these characteristics seem to flow out from the bronze or copper. Not since the days of the Roman emperors, one concludes, has personal royal glory been made so evidently incarnate. Then look again at the great painting by David of Napoleon's coronation, Joséphine prostrate at his feet, the crown raised high, the Corsican upstart in the panoply of state. Finally, look at any photograph of de Gaulle, striding down the Champs-Elysées, lofty, disdainful, outrageously sure of himself.

Louis XIV, Napoleon, de Gaulle, all heads of state, all military commanders. Perhaps there lies the secret of France's love of glory, of a characteristic which is often confused with mere chauvinism. It has very little to do with the process of law and democracy, and a great deal to do with the charisma of personality and with the cult of the warrior king (pedants would exclude de Gaulle, but he was a reigning monarch in everything except title). It also has much to do with iconography, with the way in which French rulers have wished to be portrayed. Rigaud's famous portrait of Louis XIV tells it all. He stands swathed in ermine and blue velvet stamped with gold fleurs-de-lis, his left leg thrust forward, a massive sword disappearing into his robes, crown and scepter to his right, the chain and star of the Saint-Esprit round his neck. The background is crimson, gold, and royal blue. The expression on his face is one of supreme certainty: in the future, in France, above all in himself. Curiously, though, the face barely matters. It is the trappings of monarchy which evoke *la gloire*.

Compare a Rigaud or Largillière portrait of Louis XIV, or a David or Gros portrait of Napoleon, or a Karsh photograph of de Gaulle, with a Lely Charles II, or a Gainsborough George III, or a photograph of Winston Churchill, and the difference between the French and the English approach to their respective rulers becomes immediately apparent. In the Lely portrait at Goodwood, Charles, too, like his contemporary Louis, is decked out with robes and tassels; the George hangs from his neck, and the Garter circles his left leg. But there the similarity ends. He is seated, relaxed almost, his right hand nonchalantly drooping by the crown. The interest lies in the face. Peter Stroehling's portrait of George III reveals a plump country gentleman being gazed up at by a spaniel; the Garter star seems almost out of place, the gold of the Windsor uniform a trifle vulgar. And any photograph of Churchill concentrates not on the accoutrements but on the pugnacious facial expression.

For the French, this would not be enough. They would understand the iconography of the Van Dyck portraits of Charles I, and the richness and swirl of color which Lawrence put to such effect in his treatment of George IV, without, perhaps, reflecting on the lesson of hubris and nemesis. Charles I's notion of kingship and the royal supremacy eventually provided his son and heir with a greater sense of proportion. George IV was compensating for the fact that at heart he was neither monarch nor warrior. Napoleon III, who thought of himself as emperor and military commander and was portrayed as such, reaped the whirlwind of his lust for glory in the shambles of Sedan.

Saint-Simon gives a devastating portrait of Louis XIV which sums up that quest for *la gloire* which has revealed itself so disastrously at Blenheim and Waterloo, at Borodino and Sedan, at Verdun and Dien Bien Phu. "He loved glory. . . . The poison gradually spread until it reached a degree almost unbelievable in a prince who was not unintelligent or without experience of the world. . . . He acquired a pride so colossal that, truly, had not God implanted in his heart the fear of the devil, even in his worst excesses, he would literally have allowed himself to be worshipped. What is more, he would have found worshippers; witness the extravagant monuments that have been set up to him, for example the statue in the Place des Victoires. . . . From this false pride stemmed all that ruined him."

And it was the building of Versailles which set the seal on this hubristic self-glorification. It is one of the modern wonders of the world, vast, a city more than a palace, a gigantic carapace, a monument to folly and extravagance on an unparalleled scale, an apotheosis and a disaster. It possesses none of the elegance and charm of Fontainebleau, it is grandeur writ large. One courtier called it a labyrinth; Colbert thought it vastly inferior to the Louvre. Voltaire had mixed feelings: "When you arrive at Versailles, from the courtyard side you see a wretched, top-heavy building, with a façade seven windows long, surrounded with everything which the imagination could conceive in the way of bad taste. When you see it from the garden side, you see an immense palace whose defects are more than compensated by its beauties."

But it was Saint-Simon who poured the greatest scorn and contempt on Louis's extravagance. "On the courtyard side, the constriction is suffocating and the vast wings recede quite pointlessly. On the garden front, one is able to appreciate the beauty of the building as a whole, but it looks like a palace that had been destroyed by fire because the upper storey and the roofs are still missing. The chapel towers above it because of Mansart's attempt to force the King to add an entire upper storey. As it now is, it presents the distressing appearance of some vast hearse. Everywhere in the chapel the craftsmanship is exquisite, but the design is nil, for everything was planned from the point of view of the tribune, because the King never went below." Even the greater glory of God was subservient to the glory of Louis.

The gardens are undeniably magnificent, and the use of water spectacular. But how many tourists know of the cost in resources, both financial and human? "That same lack of water brought about the destruction of the French infantry, for peace reigned at that time and M. de Louvois conceived the notion of changing the course of the Eure between Chartres and Maintenon, so as to bring that river bodily to Versailles." In Saint-Simon's account, the whole extraordinary enterprise takes on something of the building of the Pyramids.

> Who could count the gold and the men lost in an attempt which was continued for several years? They made a camp at the site of the works, and in the end it was forbidden under heavy penalties to mention the sick, or still worse, the dying, whom the hard labour and exhalations from the turned earth were taking off day by day. How many soldiers wasted long years in trying to recover their health? How many more never did recover? During the whole of that time, not only junior officers, but colonels, brigadiers, and even generals employed there, were forbidden to absent themselves a quarter of an hour, or miss so much as a quarter of an hour's duty on the site. The enterprise finally came to an end with the disastrous war of 1688. It has never been restarted. Nothing remains but shapeless mounds to perpetuate the memory of a barbarous piece of folly.

Here is glory run amok, the result justifying the means, no matter how ruinous or ill-conceived. Does Versailles then, in a word, work? It cannot but impress by its sheer size, by the ingenuity which was lavished on its construction, by the sumptuous decoration of the rooms, by the hordes of bewildered or bored tourists who throng its courtyards, its parterres, its stairways, and its corridors. It is not beautiful, though. It stuns, it astounds, it dazzles, but it does not delight. For sheer pleasure, one must turn to the Trianon, or to Fontainebleau, to buildings recognizably habitable. Like some prehistoric monster, skeletally exquisite but no longer serving any purpose except as a conglomeration on the grandest possible scale to be marveled at, out of time, out of mind, out of date, Versailles wallows in the soft French countryside. Its fountains play on, but here there are only memories: Louis XIV as impresario, organizing spectacles, and, in his salad days, amorous, charming, captivating; the revolutionary crowds pouring into the great courtyard and demanding that their King and Queen should return to the capital; the vengeful princes and margraves of Germany creating a Prussian emperor in the Galerie des Glaces; the remaking of Europe after the First World War, reconstruction leading to inevitable destruction. Perhaps Versailles is best seen as the most expensive theater in the world.

And if Versailles demonstrates architectural and kingly glory, Les Invalides exudes Napoleonic, warlike glory. There is, as I have said elsewhere, a sadness about this monument to past triumphs. But unlike Versailles, Les Invalides can be grasped. It is impressive, yes, but the mind can encompass it. Besides Napoleon himself, France's famous marshals are commemorated: Turenne; Vauban; the great fortifier Foch, whose reputation survived the holocaust of the Great War; two of Napoleon's brothers and, pathetically, his son L'Aiglon, the King of Rome. It is not excessive, though it is wholly emblematic. As John Russell has said, "The Invalides is, if not the heart of France, at any rate the heart of *la gloire*." It is also, ironically, a second bequest of Louis XIV's. His idea of glory was passed to Napoleon, and in turn to President de Gaulle's Minister for the Arts, André Malraux, who established the Musée de l'Armée there.

It must be admitted that Charles de Gaulle, too, personified *la gloire*. Exasperating, arrogant, touchy, he seemed in his elongated gawkiness a curious successor to Louis XIV (cartoonists liked to sketch him *à la dix-septième,* with full-bottomed wig and imperious stick). He annoyed his allies, who foolishly expected some gratitude or humility. He was the heaviest cross Churchill ever had to bear. He blocked Great Britain's entry into the Common Market. But he extricated France from Algeria and he had no compunction in sacrificing his former colleagues in order to preserve France. And, literally as well as figuratively, he rose head and shoulders above other contemporary world statesmen. Which, of course, is why he was so much hated.

The careers of Napoleon and de Gaulle bear comparison, though it is always unwise to take such imposed similarities too far. But nevertheless, both their careers were born out of social upheaval and military disaster. It is astonishing that Napoleon, a mere youthful artillery officer from despised Corsica, should have pulled together a country reeling from the horrors of revolution; survived the ignominy of defeat in Egypt; created a new France, constitutionally, legally, and organizationally; brought emperors and kings to their knees; allied himself through marriage with one of the proudest European dynasties; fought a series of impeccably planned and devastatingly executed campaigns; had the whole world within his grasp . . . and, so very nearly, held it there. It is equally extraordinary that Charles de Gaulle, a brilliant though suspect tank commander, should have snatched from the fall of France a personal triumph. Who else, one wonders, could have continued to assert the position of himself and his country in the face of dislike and mistrust? Who else, like Napoleon returning from Elba, could have emerged from the self-imposed exile of Colombey-les-Deux-Eglises to restore France's confidence? Both men were seized with the concept of *la gloire*. Both took that concept to the ultimate.

Of course, there is the reverse on the bright coin of glory. Few would maintain that the relentless pursuit of *la gloire* throughout most of the second half of the nineteenth century brought either long-term benefit or more than evanescent prestige to France. Colonial wars in Africa were brutal, bloody, and unnecessary. Involvement in the Crimea, in Italy, in Mexico demonstrated the simple fact that France needed to be seen to be involved. The Franco-Prussian War brought down a dynasty and bankrupted a nation. And, more recently, attempts to reinforce the sense of patriotic glory have collapsed in ludicrous colonial escapades and the destruction of a harmless ship in a New Zealand harbor. The gift of a bundle of diamonds by a self-styled African emperor with blood on his hands has little to do with *la gloire*.*

* *The gift from the Emperor Bokassa contributed to President Giscard d'Estaing's electoral failure; President Mitterrand seems untouched by the scandal of his secret service's involvement in the destruction of the* Rainbow Warrior.

There are other excesses to which the protection of the spirit of France can lead the more fervent patriot. The defense of the French language is one example of what can truthfully be called chauvinism. Many wry jokes are made about the introduction of such Anglo-Saxon horrors as *le weekend, le drugstore, le whisky-soda,* et cetera (the last phrase which someone probably objected to many centuries ago). It is all nonsense, of course. It is only a decadent or a dead language that struggles against imported words and phrases. The English have been absorbing, borrowing, or stealing—it depends on your attitude or strength of feeling—any word they took a fancy to from any language they were brought into contact with since Pope Gregory sent Augustine to bring light to the heathen. Where would we be without our "maître d'hôtel," our "gondola," our "festschrift," our "khaki"? The fact is—and it is a fact which will not delight some French—that English is a richer language than French just because it is a magpie tongue. The Académie Française has been meeting for a very long time in a ludicrous attempt to purify the language, to accept seldom, to reject frequently. The image conjured up of all these serious men (very few women) debating and dilating on the ghastly effect on the language of Ronsard, Racine, and Corneille of *le cocktail* and *le bestseller* is high comedy bordering on farce.

AN ASPECT of French law is even more startling. There is an arcane regulation called *le droit moral* (any sensible person faced with the word "moral" should run for the hills) which defies all logic. It has, though, a considerable amount to do with *la gloire.* I have personal experience of its peculiarities. The publishing company for which I work has over the years commissioned translations of virtually all Albert Camus's works. Our relations with the excellent house of Gallimard, for whom Camus once worked, have always been cordial. Alas, no more. With, as it transpired, a remarkable lack of foresight I commissioned some years ago a biography of the Nobel Prize winner. There had been previous books on Camus, both biographical and critical, in both senses of the word. It would be difficult to maintain that everything written, say, by Shakespeare or Tolstoy or Scott Fitzgerald was flawless and of general excellence; and anyone who criticized aspects of *Coriolanus* or *Anna Karenina* or *Tender Is the Night* would be unlikely to find himself in court. They arrange matters differently in France.

The *droit moral* imposes a moral right, indeed a moral obligation, on any French publisher to protect the reputation of any writer he has published, *tout court,* as they say over there. The biography of Camus which I had commissioned was, in the main, laudatory, but it cast a few aspersions: on Camus's claims of involvement with the Resistance, on his journalism, on the philosophical content of some of his plays. In other words, it was not unrelieved joy and delight. The fact that Camus emerged in a far more interesting light than in previous books was of little concern to the lawyers. Here was a flagrant case of anti-Gallic propaganda. The reputation of one of the greatest writers of the twentieth century had been traduced. The British publishers in question were clearly unfit to continue to hold the copyrights in translation of Camus's works.

The due process of the law was put in motion. Distinguished lawyers conferred, argued, shrugged their shoulders, expostulated, with, I must admit, a considerable degree of charm. English barristers are usually good value (in the theatrical context, at least), but they do not hold a candle to their French counterparts. The *avocat* in full flow is a magical sight. The resonant phrases pour forth, each eyebrow raised or hand waved is timed to a nicety, we are impressed by the argument while we are blandished by the language. If Dreyfus had been defended by this man, one thinks, the history of France would have been totally altered.

The histrionics, unfortunately, were less crucial than the law itself. After a number of years, many conferences, and a flood of telexes, a verdict was handed down. In the French courts, the defendant is assumed to be guilty and it is up to his lawyers to convince the judges otherwise. Much deliberation produced a slightly odd verdict. One of the plaintiffs, the French publisher, was deemed to have lost its case; the other accuser, the Camus estate, had triumphed. The result: punitive damages (though considerably reduced from the original demand) and the status quo on the copyrights maintained. Whether Camus's reputation had been restored by the judgment, whether indeed it had ever been damaged by the biography, these remain moot points, outside the jurisdiction of the French courts. What is certain—and the point would have produced a cynical grin on Dickens's face—is that the lawyers derived much entertainment and no little financial benefit from this curious law. There is nothing like a new precedent to cause a barrister to leap with joy like a springtime lamb.

The facts of the case are of merely incidental interest, but they do shed additional light on the French notion of *la gloire*. The inference was that foreigners had no right to denigrate the reputation, literary or historical, of a son of France. One needs to be exceedingly cautious in future. Céline was, therefore, without a shadow of doubt anti-Fascist; Proust never had homosexual relations with anyone; Malraux was indubitably not a Communist; Sartre was chaste at all times; Gide had no propensity toward seducing Arab boys; Aragon was as sane as you or I. And let us not even attempt an assessment of the nineteenth century. Balzac, Flaubert, George Sand, Verlaine, Rimbaud . . . where would it all end? Much safer to cry: *"Vive la gloire!"* It is encouraging, though, that the excellent Monsieur Chauvin, who gave his name to the French vice of chauvinism, does not feature in the pages of the Larousse encyclopedia.

Iron in the Soul

O N 14 JUNE 1940, the German army entered Paris after one of the most extraordinary and devastatingly successful campaigns in the history of warfare. It had taken the panzers of Guderian and Rommel barely a month to crush the French, to make the much-vaunted Maginot Line a term of derision, and to force Lord Gort's British Expeditionary Force into the sea.

Hitler's Order of the Day for 10 May, the eve of the Battle of France, read: "Soldiers of the West Front! The hour of the most decisive battle of the future of the German nation has come. For three hundred years it was the aim of British and French Governments to hinder every workable consolidation of Europe, and above all to keep Germany in weakness and impotence . . . Soldiers of the West Front! With this, the hour has come to you. The battle which is beginning today will decide the fate of the German nation for the next thousand years. Do your duty . . ." It was Hitler's campaign, based on his own strategy, and it was Hitler's triumph.

On 20 June, with Hess, Ribbentrop, and his army commanders beside him, he stood in a clearing in the forest at Rethondes. The exact place for the handing over of the German peace demands had been chosen with savage precision. Less than twenty-two years before, in November 1918, Foch and Weygand had presided over the humiliation of the German Empire in a railway carriage halted at Rethondes; now, the same carriage had been removed from the museum where it had rested and was about to be pressed for a second time into witnessing an act of national degradation. The memorial granite block nearby spoke of "the criminal pride of the German people." Their pride had been restored.

William Shirer, the CBS correspondent in Berlin and acute observer of the unreality of the Phony War, watched the Führer's face. "It is afire with scorn, anger, hate, revenge, triumph. He steps off the monument and contrives to make even this gesture a masterpiece of contempt. . . . He swiftly snaps his hands on his hips, arches his shoulders, plants his feet wide apart. It is a magnificent gesture of defiance, of burning contempt for this place now and all that it has stood for in the twenty-two years since it witnessed the humbling of the German Empire." A debt to history had been paid, just as the choice of the Galerie des Glaces at Versailles for Germany's acceptance of the punitive peace terms imposed upon her in 1919 was motivated by memories of that day in 1871 when Wilhelm of Prussia had himself crowned Emperor in the most hubristic display of self-aggrandizement since Napoleon wrested the crown from the Pope's hands and placed it on his own head.

Napoleon I, Wilhelm I, Napoleon III, Foch, Hitler . . . They are the historical matter, the warlords and conquerors and ultimately mere playthings of European history over a span of a century and a half. And to complete the sextet, back in Bordeaux, whither the French Government had fled, Marshal Pétain, the hero of Verdun, was the ruler—if that is the correct word—of defeated France. He was eighty-four years old. His onetime fervent admirer Charles de Gaulle had fled to England.

With the collapse of France, it seemed that history had come full circle. Shirer commented on the mood in Berlin: "The taking of Paris has . . . stirred something very deep in the hearts of most Germans. It was always a wish-dream of millions here." The great majority of French men and women felt an overpowering sense of relief; the light of common day was, at the very least, more cheering than the nightmare of war *à outrance.* And a small minority actually welcomed the victorious Germans. It is easy to see why.

DURING THE seventy years between 1870 and 1940, French territory was invaded three times, France was defeated twice and would have been defeated a third time, had it not been for the so-called miracle of the Marne when Marshal Joffre held the Germans almost from the gates of Paris after the younger, and lesser, von Moltke had tampered with the great Schlieffen plan. (Ludendorff's final big push in 1918 very nearly repeated the process.) During three wars, two of extreme brevity and one of appalling duration and cataclysmic effect, France was invaded and occupied. In the First World War, not only were large areas of her northeastern lands—stretching from the sea near Ostend right down through Arras, Soissons, and Rheims and all the way south to Mulhouse on the Swiss border—turned into a morass of mud and dead trees and barbed wire, but she had suffered such casualties as to be almost unimaginable: nearly 900,000 men killed, and a further 420,000 who died of their wounds or of the various epidemics which ran through the trenches of the Western Front.

But, before analyzing the effects of the First World War upon the collective French ethos, one must touch on the events of 1870. If ever a war was started for the most insignificant reason, then the Franco-Prussian War is the perfect exemplar. Ostensibly, the Emperor Napoleon III demanded from the King of Prussia a guarantee that he would never repeat his proposal of a Hohenzollern candidate for the vacant Spanish throne. The whole affair belonged more to the days of Louis XIV than to the second half of the nineteenth century. Wilhelm himself was perfectly prepared to be accommodating, but was so pestered by the French ambassador to Prussia and, more crucially, his resolution was so stiffened by Bismarck, that he lost patience and declined to give such an undertaking. Napoleon, for his part, recalled his easy victories over the Austrians at Magenta and Solferino eleven years previously, and chose to forget the unfortunate affair of Maximilian, the Habsburg archduke whom he had endeavored to place on the Mexican throne. Above all, the Empress Eugénie, mirroring Bismarck both in her influence and her bellicosity though sadly not in her intelligence and statecraft, urged her weak and ill husband toward the attainment of *"la gloire."* France, she said, demanded war. The press agreed. So, it seemed, did France. Napoleon declared war on Prussia on 15 July. Bismarck's exquisite plan of temptation coupled with irritation had succeeded to perfection.

Thirteen days later, Napoleon rode off to the front. His cheeks were heavily rouged in an attempt to disguise the extreme pallor caused by the pain in his bladder. He was in no fit state to sit a horse, let alone command an army utterly unprepared for war and—far worse—blissfully unaware of this unpreparedness. Maps of Germany had been issued, but no maps of France. The Prussians had at their disposal all the ingenuity and industry which the industrialist Krupp could offer and, in von Moltke, a commander of the first rank. The French were poorly armed, worse trained, and led by generals with no battle experience, men who had won their spurs in footling colonial skirmishes.

Even so, the French were convinced that they would win and win conclusively. A few dissented from this overwhelming optimism. The French ambassador in Washington warned: "You will not go to Germany, you will be crushed in France. Believe me, I know the Prussians." Then he committed suicide. And Gustave Flaubert wrote to George Sand: "I am mortified with disgust at the stupidity of my countrymen. . . . Their wild enthusiasm prompted by no intelligent motive makes me long to die, that I may be spared the sight of it." The first was dismissed as a hysteric, the second as a meddling scribbler. Both were largely ignored.

But they were right. The officers caracoling on their horses and the regiments of fine-looking soldiers in their flashy uniforms were out of a comic opera; they had no place on the battlefield. And that was how it turned out. After a few early illusory successes, the French were forced onto the defensive. All their training, and indeed their character, had given them dash and élan when they attacked. A well-organized withdrawal did not feature in their particular war manual. Soon, Bazaine's army was shut up in the fortress of Metz, and Marshal MacMahon had retreated into Sedan. General Ducrot commented crudely, *"Nous sommes dans un pot de chambre et nous y serons emmerdés!"* On the evening of 1 September, Sedan capitulated, and the following day the army consisting of over 100,000 men became prisoners of war. Napoleon himself was packed off to Germany. General de Wimpffen, who had taken over from the wounded MacMahon (it is a curious fact that so many French commanders possess such un-French names), pleaded for less harsh terms, on the basis that "rigorous measures would awaken bad passions and perhaps bring on endless war between France and Prussia." But Bismarck was unmovable.

Strasbourg fell on 27 September. On 29 October, Bazaine finally surrendered Metz; his critics maintained that he had smoked all day and played billiards all night. And the following day, the village of Le Bourget, a mere four miles from the walls of Paris, had fallen to the Prussians. The siege of Paris had effectively started on 20 September, when Versailles had surrendered and the Prussian armies had completed their encirclement.

Ironically, it could be claimed that, if Paris had capitulated

* *"We are in a chamber pot, and they will shit on us."*

immediately, future relations between France and Germany would have been wholly different; and certainly the deep bitterness caused by the atrocities committed by both sides during the period of the Commune,* when Paris faced a second revolution in many ways more savage than that of 1789, would have been alleviated. The Prussian Crown Prince saw the danger and desperately tried to influence his father (just as—history repeating itself yet again—Wilhelm II's son would endeavor to persuade *his* father that the siege of Verdun should be abandoned), but humanitarianism was a quality unlikely to be admired by the Prussian victors. Instead, the siege proceeded, the resolution of the French defenders was stiffened rather than weakened by the continuous bombardment, by danger and hunger, by the imminence of red revolution, above all by the loathing for the barbarians without the gates.

In January 1871, Bismarck's dream was realized. In Versailles's Galerie des Glaces an extraordinary ceremony took place. The princes and margraves and grand dukes were assembled for the voluntary handing over of their powers. The supremacy of the house of Hohenzollern was about to be recognized. W. H. Russell of *The Times* was there:

> It is 12 o'clock. The boom of a gun far away rolls above the voices in the Court hailing the Emperor King. Then there is a hush of expectation, and then rich and sonorous rise the massive strains of the chorale chanted by the men of regimental bands assembled in a choir, as the King, bearing his helmet in his hand, and dressed in full uniform as a German General, stalked slowly up the long gallery, and bowing to the clergy in front of the temporary altar opposite him, halted and dressed himself right and front, and then twirling his heavy moustache with his disengaged hand, surveyed the scene at each side of him.

Edmond de Goncourt noted in his diary: "That really marks the end of the greatness of France."

And, on 30 January, the siege of Paris ended. It had lasted for 130 days. After some desultory resistance in the provinces petered out, the Franco-Prussian War was over. In terms of men killed it was not a debilitating war, but in terms of national pride outraged

---

* *We owe the word "Communist" to this strange and dreadful period in the history of France, though the Commune of the French Revolution was equally to blame for giving Lenin his grand concept.*

it was a catastrophe. France had been stripped of Alsace and Lorraine, rich industrial areas but also symbols. Financial reparations amounting to £200 million were demanded, and Prussian soldiers would not leave until these had been paid. Scapegoats might be found—Napoleon III in exile; Bazaine condemned to death, a sentence commuted to life imprisonment—but the fact remained that France had suffered a crushing defeat, her armies had fought variably, often with great courage, usually without effect, sometimes not at all. Her politicians and her generals were discredited, her monarchy had been erased from the pages of history, Paris had succumbed yet again to civil war and a pattern of savage reprisals, quasi-judicial murder, and the ruthless eradication of the revolutionary spirit. It was an appalling situation, a nadir which could surely never be repeated. Edmond de Goncourt despaired as he watched the prisoners of war arriving back from Germany at the Gare du Nord with "pale faces, thin bodies in greatcoats too big for them, faded red cloth and worn gray cloth." France had indeed sunk low.

One sentiment alone held the nation together, once the Prussians had at last left in 1873, and once the smoke and blood of the Commune had begun to fade (though for Lenin and his followers it never faded). It was hatred of the Germans, a passionate desire for revenge, not just the restoration to France of Alsace and Lorraine but the humiliation of Prussia. The Crown Prince had predicted what German intransigence and lack of humanity would bring about: "The longer this struggle lasts, the better for the enemy and the worse for us. The public opinion of Europe has not remained unaffected by the spectacle. We are no longer looked upon as the innocent sufferers of wrong, but rather as the arrogant victors, no longer content with the conquest of the foe, but fain to bring about his utter ruin. No more do the French appear in the eyes of neutrals as a mendacious, contemptible nation, but as the heroic-hearted people that against overwhelming odds is defending its dearest possessions in honourable fight." And the man whose sentiments and sense were so markedly disregarded by his son, the future Kaiser Wilhelm II, ended his Cassandra-like prognostication with these telling words: "Bismarck has made us great and powerful, but he has robbed us of our friends, the sympathies of the world, and—our conscience."

Six months later, a Methodist minister, the Reverend W. Gibson, viewed the situation from the French point of view and came to an equally gloomy conclusion:

> I regret to find that the determination to seek to take their revenge sooner or later on Prussia is again manifesting itself among the Parisians. . . . Alas for France, and alas for the hope of the peace of Europe! . . . Germany, when within the next few years she again encounters France in arms, will find her a very different foe from the France of 1870; and who knows but that before the end of this century there may be a similar triumph in Paris to that which is now being celebrated in Berlin? I vainly hoped that France would feel herself fairly beaten and be willing to accept her inferior position.

Mr. Gibson anticipated too soon the opening of the First World War, but otherwise his look into the future was astonishingly accurate. In his judgment of French character he was, however, swayed by spiritual considerations entirely proper to a man of the cloth but utterly unrealistic in the circumstances. France and the honor of France had been rent asunder by war and by vicious civil strife. The treachery within—if in doubt, the French always look to the traitors among themselves and prefer to ignore the fact that disasters and defeats are often caused by external forces—had been punished. Vengeance was what mattered now.

AFTER 1870, the French thought initially of defense. The Franco-Prussian War had been a war of movement; indeed it was the sheer speed with which von Moltke's soldiers—and in particular his cavalry—had deployed that had crushed the French and turned what had appeared on paper to be an army of comparable strength into a rabble of deserters and terrified cowards. The very first act of the Etat Major de l'Armée was to commission a huge defensive system, consisting of two linked lines of sunken forts: one running from Belfort to Epinal, the second from Toul to Verdun. A gap was deliberately left between Epinal and Toul, a Venus flytrap temptingly awaiting the Prussian fly. On the face of it, this defensive line was impressive. But, as would soon transpire, it did not go far enough. The Franco-Belgian border was considered to be safe and therefore left virtually undefended except for the occasional isolated fort. And the Argonne and the Ardennes were thought to be so thick as to be impenetrable by German invaders. But the real problem lay in a fatal dichotomy in the French military mind. France was now defended, therefore the concentration should be on a war of offense. Alistair Horne, in his classic book on Verdun, *The Price of Glory,* paints a fascinating picture of military theory in the pre-1914 era:

> When the Army had fully recovered its confidence after 1870, on the completion of de Rivière's defence system, it had begun increasingly to abandon its defensive thinking. Its studies of 1870 seemed to prove convincingly that the main reason above all others for France's defeat had been the lack of offensive spirit. There was much talk about the posture of attack being most suited to the national temperament; the spirit of the *"furia francese"* was evoked from as far off as the Battle of Pavia in 1525, as was Danton's exhortation to the defenders of Verdun in 1792—*"Il nous faut de l'audace, encore de l'audace, toujours de l'audace."** The new mood was also well matched to the philosophy of Bergson that was now all the rage in France, with its emphasis on the *"élan vital."* As the years moved further away from the actual experience of war, so the philosophy of the offensive moved ever further from reality.

Little study was made of the effective use of defense during the American Civil and the Boer wars. The idea of breaking off an attack in order to consolidate a position, to dig in and prepare for a counterattack, was anathema to the supporters of the grand new theory perpetrated by the aptly named Colonel de Grandmaison, head of operations on the General Staff. *"L'attaque à outrance"*—attack to the bitter end—was the battle cry.

All this has much to say about the French character—the impulsiveness, the dislike of anything that smacked of withdrawal however organized, the bravura and bravado, the lack of analysis, the insensate courage, Cyrano's panache—but it says rather less for the intelligence of the High Command. Grandmaison's theories seem in retrospect to border on lunacy: total reliance on the bayonet attack; ground lost to be regained without delay without thought of casualties; contempt for heavy artillery; the same attitude toward air power or reconnaissance, and even toward the

---

* *"We must have boldness, still more boldness, always boldness."*

machine gun. One of his tenets went as follows: "For the attack only two things are necessary: to know where the enemy is and to decide what to do. What the enemy intends to do is of no consequence." Attack, attack, attack, the word echoes and reverberates. Any loss of courage, however overwhelming the odds against, would be dealt with rigorously. In the days before shell shock and battle fatigue became part of the language, court-martial and summary execution awaited the slightest deviation from the *attaque à outrance*.

For France, the First World War started disastrously . . . and predictably. Her soldiers streamed into Alsace and were mown down by the despised German machine guns. The cavalry, in full dress uniform, fell from their horses in their hundreds. It was like the slaughter of the heavily encumbered French knights destroyed by Henry V's bowmen at Agincourt. As had happened in the past, and would happen again in the future, France was fighting the wrong war at the wrong time with the wrong weapons. Courage was not enough. As Alistair Horne puts it, "The French stubble-fields became transformed into gay carpets of red and blue." It seemed as if Paris would fall twice within the space of forty-four years, until Joffre and Gallieni performed the "miracle of the Marne." By the end of 1914, the lines of trenches lay from Switzerland to the Channel, the war of mobility was over, the war of attrition had begun. And, during those five months, France had lost 300,000 men killed and twice that number missing presumed dead, wounded, or taken prisoner.

Far worse was to come. On the Eastern Front, Russia was heading toward total defeat. Gallipoli and the struggle for the Dardanelles emerged as nothing better than a brutal mirage. The great British fleet lay at anchor at Scapa, and the German submarines sank essential supply ships seemingly at will. The German High Command decided that if the French could be crushed once and for all, the war would soon be ended. General Erich von Falkenhayn, the new chief of the General Staff, composed a memorandum for the Kaiser in December 1915. It was a fateful document, the basis of destruction for both Germans and French, though it was founded on a highly intelligent appreciation of the general situation. Von Falkenhayn argued, correctly, that the British were less than committed to the Western Front and that Tsarist Russia was crumbling away.

There remains only France. . . . If we succeeded in opening
the eyes of her people to the fact that in a military sense they
have nothing more to hope for, that breaking point would be
reached and England's best sword knocked out of her hand.
To achieve that object the uncertain method of a mass break-
through, in any case beyond our means, is unnecessary. We
can probably do enough for our purposes with limited resources. Within our reach behind the French sector of the
Western Front there are objectives for the retention of which
the French General Staff would be compelled to throw in
every man they have. If they do so the forces of France will
bleed to death . . . whether we reach our goal or not.

It was an utterly callous strategy. Choose a vital point in the
enemy's defenses, one which must be defended at all costs, for military and patriotically nationalistic reasons, and slowly, gradually,
ineluctably drain the enemy of his manpower, bleed him white.
Callous the strategy may have been, but it was a masterly plan,
provided only that the attackers were not likewise forced to bleed
to death. But von Falkenhayn envisaged a more immediate death
for the French, and he knew where he should slash the artery.
"The objectives of which I am speaking now are Belfort and Verdun. The considerations urged above apply to both, yet the preference must be given to Verdun."

Verdun. Like Passchendaele and the Somme, like Stalingrad,
like Dien Ben Phu, perhaps like Vietnam, the name stands as a
memorial to waste, to the destruction of a generation, to the re-
fusal of military commanders to think of their soldiers as human
beings, to the utter futility of war. And perhaps Verdun is the
worst of all these, not merely because of the literally unbelievable
casualty lists but because of the horrors of warfare which would
have made Goya blench and turn aside. The numbers of men
killed or wounded need to be stated: On the French side, they vary
from between 377,000 and 469,000; on the German side, from between 337,000 and 373,000. And these figures take no account of
casualties on the Verdun front before or after the ten-month siege.

But it is the effect of Verdun, the experience of Verdun, on
and by the survivors which is relevant here. The countless acts of
blind bravery, as the conflict ebbed and flowed around Fort Douaumont and Le Mort Homme, the Bois des Caures and Fort
Vaux, are all to be found in Alistair Horne's history of the battle.

But something of the atmosphere must be conveyed, if only to show how the seeds of 1940 were sown in the mud of Verdun.

A German student, writing in June 1916, just before he was killed, referred to the fighting at Verdun as "war in its most appalling form." He was right. A French lieutenant observed the effect on his regiment as it staggered away from Douaumont:

> First came the skeletons of companies occasionally led by a wounded officer, leaning on a stick. All marched, or rather advanced in small steps, zigzagging as if intoxicated. . . . It was hard to tell the colour of their faces from that of their tunics. Mud had covered everything, dried off, and then another layer had been re-applied. . . . They said nothing. They had even lost the strength to complain. . . . It seemed as if these mute faces were crying something terrible, the unbelievable horror of their martyrdom. Some Territorials who were standing near me became pensive. They had that air of sadness that comes over one when a funeral passes by, and I overheard one say: "It's no longer an army! These are corpses!" Two of the Territorials wept in silence, like women.

Images of the First World War have become almost commonplace: lines of blind soldiers, their eyes bandaged; the bodies, nearly dead but not quite, twitching on the barbed wire; the skeletal trees and the craters and the rat-infested trenches; the walls of the dugouts supported by corpses; the swirling clouds of mustard gas; the dead horses, their teeth bared in a last grimace; the thousands upon thousands of men thrown away for the sake of a few yards gained or lost, it hardly seemed to matter. All this is known, recorded, true. But how much more ghastly was Verdun! It was at Verdun that phosgene gas was first used. It was at Verdun that flamethrowers were first used. Both these weapons of modern civilization seemed like inventions from hell; the endless bombardment from the German heavy artillery completed the picture of inferno.

But the French, even more perhaps than the British or the Germans, had also to contend with their generals. Joffre, de Castelnau, Mangin "the Butcher," and Nivelle—let alone all those who were packed off to Limoges out of harm's way, so that a new word, *limoger,* was introduced into the language—had forgotten that a soldier was not just a fighting machine but also a human being who experienced fear and hunger and pain. Only Pétain, significantly, expressed sympathy or sorrow for the sufferings of the ordinary soldiers, the *poilus*. "How depressing it was when they returned" from what he called the "furnace of Verdun," Pétain noted, "whether singly as wounded or footsore stragglers, or in the ranks of companies impoverished by their losses! Their expressions, indescribably, seemed frozen by a vision of terror; their gait and their postures betrayed a total dejection; they sagged beneath the weight of horrifying memories; when I spoke to them, they could hardly reply, and even the jocular words of the old soldiers awoke no echo from their troubled minds." Joffre would not even pin a medal on a wounded soldier, so disturbed was he by the sight. Like so many of the second-rate butcher-commanders of the Western Front, he felt his duty lay in appearing always imperturbable: a good night's sleep, never under any circumstances to be disturbed, and two gargantuan meals a day was his recipe for success.

No wonder the French soldiers mutinied. The holocaust of Verdun came to an end in July 1916. Alistair Horne says:

> Between February 21 and July 15, the French had lost over 275,000 men (according to their official war history) and 6,563 officers. Of these, somewhere between 65,000 and 70,000 had been killed; 64,000 men and 1,400 officers had been captured. Over 120,000 of the French casualties had been suffered in the last two months alone. On the German side, Falkenhayn's "limited offensive" had already cost close to a quarter of a million men; equivalent to about twice the total complement of the nine divisions he had been willing to allocate for the battle in February. The German artillery had fired off approximately 22,000,000 rounds; the French perhaps 15,000,000. Out of their total of ninety-six divisions on the Western Front, the French had sent seventy to Verdun; the Germans forty-six and a half.

But it was, of course, not the end. Though the British increasingly took the major share of the futile series of costly offensives during 1916 and 1917, General Nivelle was preparing one last catastrophe for the French armies. The slaughter on the Chemin des Dames was the point beyond which they refused to go. Mutiny seemed about to turn into revolution, the Commune revived. Field Marshal Haig said that he had heard that 30,000 mutineers had been "dealt with." Only Pétain could restore order. He succeeded in this almost impossible task, but it was, as Sergeant Marc Boasson said, in a sense too late: "Pétain has purified the unhealthy atmosphere. But it will be difficult for him to wipe out the impression of defiance which now rests in the heart of the soldier towards those whom he should have considered his leaders, his guides, his protectors, his paternal friends. . . . They have ruined the heart of the French soldier."

At the end of the First World War, France—much like Britain after the Second World War—was victorious but exhausted. She had avenged the defeats of 1870, but at an appalling cost. Alsace and Lorraine were wrested back, and punitive terms were imposed on the defeated Germans by the peace treaty at Versailles. The French, like the Bourbons, had learned nothing and forgotten nothing. Communism was in the air. A new anti-British feeling had been growing strongly, based on the widely held belief that the troops contributed by the British Empire had not pulled their weight (*"ces sales khakis"* was a not uncommon term of abuse).

But, more than any other event, it was Verdun which entered, like corrosive metal, into the soul of France. One young officer voiced the feeling with passion: "They will not be able to make us do it again another day; that would be to misconstrue the price of our effort. They will have to resort to those who have not lived out these days." A lieutenant in the artillery agreed: "This war has marked us for generations. It has left its imprint upon our souls. All those inflamed nights of Verdun we shall rediscover one day in the eyes of our children." And Sergeant Boasson wrote with the greatest fury: "This is not heroism. It is ignominy. What kind of a nation will they make of us tomorrow, these exhausted creatures, emptied of blood, emptied of thought, crushed by superhuman fatigue?"

The fatalism of the inter-war years was born in the blast furnace of Verdun.

IT IS DIFFICULT to find very much to admire about French attitudes, and above all French policies, in the flippant, nervous twenty years which separated the end of the First World War and the beginning of the Second (the same can, of course, be said with equal force about Britain). France had triumphed, but large stretches of her countryside lay devastated. France had conquered, but she had lost too many men, too tragically. The great victory

parade in Paris and the arraignment of Germany at Versailles provided little more than superficial gloss; they offered scant comfort
to the millions of women in their black dresses of mourning. Alis
tair Horne gives the economic facts and figures:

> France had expended some 25 per cent of her national for-
> tune; almost 7 per cent of her territory had been devastated
> by war, including some of the richest industrial areas; 3¼
> million hectares (12,500 square miles, or roughly the area of
> Holland) of fertile soil had been ravaged; 3,500 miles of rail-
> way and over 30,000 miles of roads were destroyed; coal pro-
> duction was down by 37 per cent compared with 1914, steel
> by 60 per cent; the trade deficit had risen from 1½ million to
> 17½ million francs. France's Ministry of Finance estimated
> the material damage caused by the Germans, and which
> would be the basis for reparations, at 134,000 million gold
> francs, a staggering figure compared with 5,000 million which
> Germany had demanded, and got, from France in 1871.

France looked for help from her erstwhile allies and from the
defeated enemy, and she looked in vain. The United States of
America withdrew into isolationism and a determination never
again to become involved in the squalid quarrels of the Old
World, which the Americans saw as both morally and economically
bankrupt. Britain, who, like France, had left a generation on the
killing fields of Flanders and the Western Front, was preoccupied
with her own internal problems. Russia had fallen to the Commu-
nists, the least likely government to look with favor on the bourgeois capitalists who less than forty years before had suppressed
the Commune with such brutality. And Germany simply could
not pay the bill. She defaulted in 1923, the French occupied the
Ruhr, the precarious German economy collapsed, and the rise of
Nazism was but a goosestep away.

It seemed as if France was falling into a kind of torpor. The
birthrate remained static (whereas the German birthrate soared).
Alsace-Lorraine had been recovered, so there was no longer a great
symbol to fight for. The old political issues were dead. The common fear was directed against the rising tide of Marxism. There
was an intense and understandable anti-war and anti-military feeling in the air; Henri Barbusse's novel *Le Feu,* which graphically
evoked the horrors of war, was a vast best-seller and a pervasive
influence on an entire generation. And the politicians hardly set

a good example. Governments fell almost weekly during the 1930s; some were brought down by scandal, most by internal wrangling, a few simply because the actors in the charade had decided to reshuffle the cast. There is a nice, shocking, possibly exaggerated story of Georges Bonnet and Camille Chautemps meeting at a lunch party. The current government had just fallen, and a new Prime Minister must be appointed. Bonnet: "It's my turn!" Chautemps: "No, Georges, it's mine!" Even poor Léon Blum, leader of the Front Populaire, and an honest man among dilettante wolves, could not stand the pace or the rabid hatred of his political rivals. Even the strongest politician seemed to be manipulated by his mistress; the salon and the bedroom held far greater influence than the cabinet office.

One need not be surprised that military thinking during this period was uncoordinated and ineffectual. General Beaufre gives a crisp description of an anarchic setup: "At the Ministry of War, the General commanded in theory, but had not the money, the administration, the personnel or the equipment; the Permanent Secretary had the money and the administration, without the responsibility of command; the various departments had personnel and equipment, but neither money nor command. The Minister stood at the head of all this, but could achieve nothing without obtaining unison from the whole orchestra, the complexity of which helped to paralyse all initiatives. The ensemble possessed only one force—that of inertia."

In Germany, an officer called Heinz Guderian published a book with the uncompromising title *Achtung—Panzer!* and in England Captain Basil Liddell Hart was formulating his theory of warfare. In France, it is true, Major Charles de Gaulle wrote a book called *Vers l'Armée de Métier,* which stressed the potential of the armored division, but he was promptly struck from the promotion list. These newfangled views were not to be tolerated by a High Command obsessed with one thing and one thing only: defense.

In 1922, an Army commission led by Marshal Joffre, who had re-emerged from the twilight of disgrace, visited Verdun and was deeply impressed by the visible signs of how well the various forts had stood up to the German artillery bombardment. Gradually they talked themselves into a pathetic fallacy: that if a proper line of fortifications, a continuous front, could be constructed, then

France could never again be invaded. Pétain, now Inspector General of the Army, agreed with this assessment. Still haunted by his experiences at Verdun, and by the wholesale slaughter of French soldiers, he lent his authority to the ultimate vision of static, defensive warfare. Like a child menaced by imaginary dragons, he wanted to pull the bedclothes over his head. In this case, however, the dragons were all too real.

On 4 January 1930, the French National Assembly voted enthusiastically for funds to be devoted to a great defensive wall stretching the length of the frontier from Basel to Longwy at the junction of the Belgian, French, and Luxembourg borders. The Minister of War was André Maginot, a veteran of Verdun. The fortifications would be called the Maginot Line in his honor. As a piece of construction, it was remarkable. Whole armies could live underground in total safety. The commissariat arrangements were finely tuned so as to avoid the dreadful difficulties which had beset the defenders of Verdun. But there were also glaring defects in the strategy. The line was too long and therefore too unwieldy; conversely, it did not possess enough depth. Then, the expense was crippling: 7,000 million francs had been expended on eighty-seven miles by 1935. More crucial still, the Belgian border was excluded from the plan, partly because the money was not available, partly because the construction of forts in that area would have disrupted industrial output. The French theorists considered that the risk of a lightning attack by an enemy across the Belgian frontier was minimal, simply because Belgium was bound to stand and fight as she had done in 1914.

But the most debilitating effect of the Maginot mentality was psychological. As Alistair Horne puts it, "Like the lotus-eating mandarins of Cathay behind their Great Wall, the French Army allowed itself to atrophy, to lapse into desuetude." Men forced to live underground, particularly during the piping days of peace, become easily bored, and morale inevitably deteriorates; maneuvers and training go by the board; an atmosphere of impregnability leads to tedium, and tedium descends to the fatal French accidie. Officers and men alike imitated Marshal Bazaine by smoking all day and playing billiards all night.

While the military lulled themselves into a totally false sense of security, and while the politicians executed their ritual dance steps and listened to their mistresses' advice, a new, fiercer spirit was abroad in the land. The seizure of power by Hitler had alarmed remarkably few people. To many he appeared as a kind of modern Hercules preparing to cleanse the Augean Stables. He was admired and imitated, and nowhere more fervently than in France. François Coty, the man who founded his fortune on the brilliant marketing of cheap scent, started a newspaper, *L'Ami du Peuple,* whose forthright slogan read: "With Hitler against Bolshevism." The great mass of the bourgeoisie was united by two sentiments: a passionate dread of Communism and an equally passionate longing for *la gloire,* as symbolized in the heroism of Verdun. They loathed and despised the politicians, both the dishonest ones in the center and the more upright ones on the left. They nursed a distrust of England, and were in general deeply anti-Semitic. Mavericks like Colonel Casimir de la Rocque and ideological theorists like Charles Maurras played on the memories and fears of the middle classes and of the survivors of the First World War. The Camelots du Roi, the Croix de Feu, the Solidarité Française, the Jeunesses Patriotes, the Action Française, all the various leagues and groups of men, some of whom were genuine patriots, some out-and-out Fascists, the great majority disaffected and above all angry, emphasized a general feeling that, of all the possible threats to France, Hitler was by no means the most dangerous; and that many of the actions of both Hitler and Mussolini could be copied to advantage.

The accession to power of Léon Blum's Front Populaire merely increased this right-wing fervor. Blum was considered by many to be a second Lenin, and the slogan "Rather Hitler than Blum" was coined in all seriousness by men of apparently liberal persuasions. Hitler's personal envoy in Paris, Otto Abetz, encouraged the deep-seated fears of the bourgeoisie. He gave financial help to any newspaper, politician, or organization prepared to air right-wing, anti-Semitic, pro-Catholic, pro-monarchy views. He frequented the political salons, he blandished and charmed. By sleight of hand he convinced men and women in positions of the greatest power and influence that Herr Hitler wished above all for peace and for a lasting rapprochement with France, so distressingly abandoned by her former ally Britain and so fundamentally weakened by Jewish speculators. An illusory, but strong because credible, Fifth Column had been conjured up virtually out of thin air.

When Neville Chamberlain returned from Munich in 1938,

he was greeted with acclaim, but above all with relief. These sentiments were even more pronounced when Edouard Daladier alighted
from his plane at Le Bourget. Simone de Beauvoir remembered
"a great wave of rejoicing" which swept over France; "I felt I had
escaped death, now and forever." The French did not want to go
to war; they did not want to be dragged into a conflict on behalf
of Czechoslovakia, or Danzig, or Poland; they did not want to be
coerced by an England which had suddenly rediscovered a conscience. Nor were they prepared for such a war. As was shortly to
become all too sadly evident, the much-vaunted Maginot Line was
irrelevant. Belgium's feckless attempt to retain her neutrality exposed the barren nature of French strategic thought. Too few officers had read Guderian's *Achtung—Panzer!*

Accounts of the final days before the fall of France make depressing reading. Paul Reynaud, already a broken man, summons
up every last vestige of energy; Churchill's offer of a "Declaration
of Union" is thrown out by the French Cabinet; a last-minute plea
for support from President Roosevelt fails; the Comtesse de Portes,
Reynaud's mistress, urges him to seek an armistice; the politicians
who are about to become collaborators—Laval, Bonnet, Baudouin—
wait for the inevitable. Edward Spears, who was about to assist
Charles de Gaulle out of France and toward his personal assump-
tion of *la gloire,* observed the total collapse of morale, and the
enormous relief which seized the country when Reynaud handed
over the reins of office to Marshal Pétain. Everyone, Spears felt,
was saying, "He will save us as he did at Verdun."

IT IS EASY to denigrate the record of France, politically and mili-
tarily, in 1940. When liberation came in 1944, all too many fingers
were pointed at the guilty men, and women. There is no more de-
plorable sight than the settling of old scores, the petty revenges,
the cruel pillorying of weak and often innocent victims. Shame
breeds guilt, and guilt can only be assuaged by deflecting it on to
others. In 1944, many people throughout France felt guilty, and
the shaved heads of women who had slept with Wehrmacht officers, the disgrace of actors and entertainers and writers who had
continued to follow their callings, the trials and executions and
reprisals, all these helped the virtuous majority to forget that their
virtue was, perhaps, somewhat tarnished. Pétain, in a moving
speech at his trial, made a similar point: "When I had earned

rest, I did not cease to devote myself to her [France]. I responded to all her appeals, whatever was my age or my weariness. She had turned to me on the most tragic day of her history. I neither sought nor desired it. I was begged to come. I came. Thus I inherited a catastrophe of which I was not the author. . . . History will tell all that I spared you, whereas my adversaries think of reproaching me for what was inevitable."

It was inevitable. The energy and willpower of France had been fatally sapped by the First World War, above all by Verdun. The shenanigans of the politicians in the 1920s and 1930s merely exacerbated a situation which already existed. The paucity and poverty of strategic analysis was a hangover from Verdun. The importance of Verdun can never be underestimated.

But we must ask the question: Should France be blamed for surrendering in 1940; should the many, many French men and women who coexisted happily enough beside the German occupiers be blamed? The answer, surely, is no. Many British and Americans, comfortable in their ignorance of what an effect war being waged in your own country can have in terms of morale and self-confidence, have castigated what they see as an inherent degeneracy in French moral fiber in 1940, a cowardice which turned into collaborationism. It is a very lofty and complacent view, which presupposes that something quite different would have occurred if it had been Britain or the United States which had been invaded three times, had been utterly humiliated once, had barely survived the second experience, and was unprepared for the third struggle.

That the French were deluded into thinking that Hitler was a man of peace and reason is incontrovertible. But the French, alas, are easily deluded. It was so in 1870, it was so in 1916, it was so in 1940. They are also curiously prone to extremes of temperament: energy followed by lassitude. The spirit of Verdun created both; it was the iron in the soul of France—for good or for evil.

xiii

Clichés and Chauvinism

XENOPHOBIA IS the unacceptable face of prejudice. It is also one of the most pleasurable and corrupting of prejudices. Everyone enjoys sneering at everyone else in the global conglomerate of disunited nations. The British are stereotyped as cold and reserved, the men ineradicably tainted by a fondness for flagellation and sodomy inculcated at their public schools, inexpert lovers of the opposite sex, passionate lovers of domestic animals and equally passionate destroyers of wild ones, democrats groping in the fog of militant trade unionism. The Italians are charming cowards, who will fleece you with a smile and run away in a battle, much given to grandiose buildings, the seduction of female students, Catholic hysteria, and the playing of roles. The Americans are larger-than-life vulgarians, their taste buds dulled by frozen drinks, their lower limbs wrapped in plaids outrageous enough to bring on apoplexy in a Highland chieftain, cameras always at the ready as they wing desperately from country to country accumulating post-cards and souvenirs and abysmal ignorance. The Germans are efficient and ruthless and bullet-headed and leather-shorted. Et cetera, et cetera.

But is there a nation that has attracted the iron filings of fixed ideas more lavishly than France? And is there a nation that cares less? The first postwar edition of the sublime *Nouveau Petit Larousse Illustré* (motto: A dictionary without examples is a skeleton) defines the word *cliché* as a metal plate used by an engraver or etcher; as a negative photographic image; and—"*fig. et fam.*"—as a commonplace, a banality, something endlessly repeated without variation.

Banalities about the French have indeed bitten so deep into the metal that it has become almost impossible to discern the light and shadow, to catch the subtle variations and nuances. The cleaning of an old painting always has its dangers. The patina of age, however encrusted, may seem more attractive than the bright new colors of the restored original. An excessive use of the cleaning fluid may even destroy forever some tiny but vital detail. This book has attempted to remove the clichés, without removing the character, to conjure up the spirit of place and people, to blend a love of France and the French with a cool realization of the defects in the national character, at least the defects as I see them.

So what about the clichés? Are the French grasping and rude and chauvinistic? Are they immoral or amoral? Are they Voltairean cynics or merely Voltairean realists? What of their reputation as lovers and cooks? Do they worship God or Mammon? Is chic exclusive to the French? Is the French language sacred? Is the French passion for *le sport* excessive? Are French composers incapable of writing serious symphonies and concertos? Is France the most beautiful country in the world? Are the French different?

I have tried to give impressions and a few facts. It is a canvas divided improbably into three: the classical energy of a Poussin, the romantic panache of a Delacroix, the shimmering haze of a

Monet. And the overall effect is sadly trite: the French are no more avaricious, lustful, greedy, slothful, or covetous than the next nation. Proud, however, they are. And they have much to be proud of. They have always been—and still are—the best cooks in the world. But it is not just the ability to create new dishes or new styles of cuisine which marks the French, it is a natural inborn appreciation of food and the effect of food. It need not be complicated or rich, it can be what some would call peasant fare, but it is good.

In the world of fashion, too, Paris has always exercised an astonishing influence. In 1850, there were 158 couturiers listed in Paris; by 1872 this figure had risen to 684, and by 1895 to 1,636. By that year, it was calculated, 400,000 people were employed in the fashion industry. Ironically, it was an Englishman, Charles Worth, who revolutionized women's clothes, but—like Molyneux after him—he had to go to Paris in order to do so. He created the myth and the reality that Paris was the center of the universe in matters of taste and style, and that any new range of clothes created there would be copied in London or New York or Saint Petersburg.

Paris has never lost its position in the league table of fashion, except for a brief period in the 1960s when the ephemeral designs of London's King's Road leapt to prominence. The list of designers of haute couture—many of them still operating—is an impressive one: Balmain, Fath, Grès, Chanel, Dior. Their shows—and those put on by their successors like Yves Saint Laurent—have always received maximum press coverage. It really seemed to matter what the new styles would be, even though the clothes on display were intended for a tiny minority of rich women and for the color plates of fashion magazines. But, nevertheless, the extraordinary fact is that after the Second World War, Dior, by creating his New Look, persuaded an entire generation of women to discard the clothes which they had painstakingly collected with their hard-won coupons. And today Paris is still the mecca of the fashion-conscious, though the couturiers are as likely to have Spanish, German, or Japanese names as French ones.

And the importance of Paris for women does not stop with clothes. Most of the houses which design clothes also design scents, so that Patou and Dior and Grès are equally famous for those bottles of expensive essences as they are for their dresses and coats.

Hermès is, for many people, synonymous with scarves. And the *instituts de beauté* flourish. Throughout the world, women buy makeup and body preparations by the ton. These products are expensive, and these days the manufacturers emphasize the purity of the contents. One firm, Clarins, offers its customers an unprecedented range of services, guaranteeing to transmit any query or complaint to any one of the following: *"laboratoire de recherche; laboratoire de contrôle; laboratoire de fabrication; ingénieur-chimiste; pharmacien; dermatalogue; biologiste; bactériologiste; centre de traitements; kinésithérapeute; cosmétologue; esthéticienne."* Its products are "serious products, efficacious, suitable for the most demanding." You know where you are the minute the French use the word *sérieux.*

Advertising in the cosmetic industry is taken extremely seriously. The copy must strike a delicate balance between art and science, as the following example shows: "The three Face-Treatment Creams with Plant Extracts are delicate and rich emulsions, which do not stick, and leave an invisible protective film on the skin that facilitates the application of makeup. Rich in specially selected ingredients, they contribute to nourish the skin, normalize the skin pH value and leave the epidermis supple and satin-smooth. Triple protection against: UVA-UVB rays, dehydration, pollution." It is perhaps doubtful whether many women have the faintest idea what their skin pH value might be, let alone know the difference between a UVA and a UVB ray, but it is all very comforting. And the choice between the three creams is an exciting one. If you have dry or, perish the thought, extra-dry skin, you should opt for a cream containing extracts of sandalwood, ginkgo biloba, red poppy, peach, camomile, and moringa. Oily skin demands a mixture of lotus, witch hazel, grapefruit, sage. And if, God help you, you suffer from lifeless, tired skin, rush for a cream containing an exotic mélange of orchid, cucumber, horsetail, and pineapple.

It is easy to mock this high-flown jargon and these bizarre concoctions, but no doubt they work. In any case, it is a very profitable business. And it is a business with its heart in Paris.

So we now have the supremely well dressed woman, strolling down the Rue du Faubourg Saint-Honoré, her face transformed by Clarins's cosmetics, her body clad in a little number from Lanvin, shoes from Charles Jourdan, a scarf and bag from Hermès, scented by Patou's Joy. But what of her mind? No doubt, she will have read the winner of the Prix Goncourt, perhaps the winner of the Renaudot or the Fémina Vie Heureuse. The French are said to be voracious readers and intellectual snobs. Certainly, they have a unique institution which governs their reading habits. It is a television program called *Apostrophes*. It has a vast and avid audience, and what its presenter, Bernard Pivot, says takes on the potency of holy writ. It is impossible to imagine a similar program lasting more than a few weeks in London or New York, and, because it is so very French, it is worth analyzing.

Pivot gathers together in a bare studio, which resembles a warehouse rather than the usual comfortable theater of the BBC or NBC, three or four people, usually writers whose latest books have just appeared. (They have all had to read one another's books.) There are no frills, they just sit around a table . . . and talk. There is no attempt to lighten the atmosphere by inserting clips showing the writer in question walking through the French countryside communing with his muse, or sitting in his publisher's office discussing editorial points, or being mobbed by frenzied fans in Brentano's or some other bookshop. They talk, Pivot prompts and prods, and they talk, for over an hour. It is extraordinarily *sérieux* and quirky and French. And it is effective. An English novelist, unknown in France, once appeared on *Apostrophes* and was astounded to see Pivot turn to the camera and announce to his millions of viewers that the man had written a great novel, and that he, Pivot, would recompense any purchaser of the book who disagreed with him. When asked subsequently how many people had taken up his offer, Pivot remembered the number as five, all of whom lived in one of the richest *arrondissements* and all of whom demanded their money back a few weeks before Christmas.

Literary novels, translated novels, even poetry have suddenly become far more popular. It was not always so. Theodore Zeldin quotes the findings of a survey carried out in 1961 to discover which were the greatest best-sellers of the century. The *Petit Larousse,* unsurprisingly, came out on top with 25 million copies sold since 1906. The ten books which had sold over a million copies each were a curious collection: Saint-Exupéry's *Vol de Nuit* and Alain-Fournier's *Le Grand Meaulnes;* the *Diary of Major Thompson,* Pierre Daninos's satirical view of both the French and the British; two foreign novels, by Irwin Shaw and Frank G. Slaughter; a book of poems by Paul Geraldy, a pious biography, the *Book of Hymns and Psalms,* Marie-Anne Desmarets's vast sentimental novel *Torrents,* published back in 1895, and her *Tin-Tin.* Rostand's *Cyrano de Bergerac,* Closterman's war novel *Le Grand Cirque,* and two more of Saint-Exupéry's novels were just short of the million mark. Françoise Sagan's *Bonjour Tristesse* and Margaret Mitchell's *Gone With the Wind* had sold over 800,000 copies; and Malraux's *La Condition Humaine,* Camus's *La Peste,* and Vercors's *Silence de la Mer* over 700,000. Gide, Proust, and Zola were well down the list.

And in 1966 there was another survey, conducted among conscripts to the armed forces. They were asked to name five authors. In order of popularity, the list read as follows: Victor Hugo, La Fontaine, Dumas, Molière, Daudet, Voltaire, Saint-Exupéry, Racine, and Lamartine. There is a distinct whiff of the classroom about these names. No doubt, in any case, the conscripts were more interested in football teams and who was likely to win the Tour de France.

With sport, one approaches a way of life rather than a mere pastime. The French are extremely *sérieux* about sports and games. An international rugby match or a vital football game will arouse wild passion. Cockfighting in the *département* of the Nord was a total craze, just as bullfighting was in the South. So, too, was hunting at the other end of the scale. Tennis, the *jeu de paume,* originated in France, and the Dauphin annoyed Henry V by sending him some tennis balls. Hockey derives from *hoquet,* a particularly violent game played by the Bretons. *Boules* and *pétanque* are highly competitive, though originally, as Zeldin says, "they were essentially an alternative to immobile drinking in cafés." Rugby football is closely related to a game called *la soule,* which dates from the twelfth century and was played with a ball made of wood or leather, twice as large as its modern equivalent, and filled with hay or air. Sometimes up to a thousand people were involved and the game went on all day. *La soule* was not for the fainthearted. Zeldin quotes an early nineteenth-century description: "It is not an ordinary amusement but a heated and dramatic game in which the players fight, strangle each other and smash each other's heads . . . a game that allows one to kill an enemy without losing one's right to Eastern communion, provided one takes care to strike as though by accident. . . . Blood flows . . . a sort of frenetic drunkenness seizes the players, the instincts of wild beasts seem to be aroused in the hearts of men, the thirst for murder seizes their throats, drives them on and blinds them. . . . Compared to it," Zeldin adds, "American football was child's play." He might have said the same about the newer forms of football and cricket as practiced by the West Indians.

All these sports have been—and many still are—pursued with passion and a high degree of competitiveness bordering on violence. When the French are at play, they perform *à outrance,* whether they are fishing, slaughtering small birds, or merely going to the races. Distinguished writers have felt it necessary to support this craze for *le sport.* Jean Giraudoux, who was to be tainted with accusations of Nazi sympathies, would certainly have approved the activities of the Hitlerjugend. Sport, according to the playwright, was "the art by which man liberates himself from himself. . . . Every human with a dull, bent or obese body is in some sense a beggar." Pierre Loti, the great adventurer, approved mightily of gymnastics. And Georges Duhamel thought it necessary to make his position clear, after he had been criticized for his dislike of spectator sports: "I have walked across half of Europe with a haversack on my back. I can, like any reasonable man, swim, ride a bicycle, drive a car, wield a racket and even row. I have for years used fencing as an exercise. I do not disdain physical exercise: I love it, I recommend it, I often long for it as part of a studious retirement."

Duhamel mentions cycling, and it is this sport which takes pride of place in its Frenchness. For a short time every year, the entire nation, it seems, is galvanized by the Tour de France. There is nothing new in this. Theodore Zeldin mentions a certain Edmond Jacquelin, a baker from Ménilmontant, who was champion of France in 1896; his "success made him so rich that he travelled around in a carriage with top hat and white gloves and had a box at the Comédie-Française." Nemesis struck. He made a number of unfortunate investments, including large sums poured into his own invention of a street-cleaning tricycle, and sank into poverty. Other champions were far more successful and luckier. In the 1980s, the winner of the Tour de France can become a millionaire through the various franchises and advertising waiting for any triumphant—and preferably charismatic—sportsman.

The mystique of the Tour de France is a powerful one. Any innocent tourist who is unlucky enough to coincide with its progress will rue the day. The roads become inundated with television crews and radio interviewers; hotels for miles around are commandeered; cafés are given over to talk exclusively on the events of the day and the likely outcome of the next day's run. Who will be wearing the coveted yellow jersey, the modern equivalent of the crusader's surcoat? Passions flare. Accusations of skulduggery rend the air. The café owner rubs his hands and waits for next year. The caravanserai passes on. Tour mania ceases. A great many people have been enriched by gambling and sponsorship. The Tour de France is a marathon for the cyclists; but for the manufacturers of bicycles, sports clothes, soft drinks, anything which can be seen and identified on television, it is a bonanza.

THE FRENCH attitude toward sport, literature, and fashion is highly individual, in short very French, very *sérieux*. But what of that greatest cliché of them all, the accusation of chauvinism? The French, it cannot be denied, have a very keen sense of their own apartness. I have already mentioned the phenomenon of *la gloire*. It can be personal—in every Frenchman's makeup there is a vestige of Louis XIV's *L'état, c'est moi*—or it can be national. French presidents and French governments still prefer to take a different line on international affairs, and seem not to care a jot about criticism. If a ship is blown up in Auckland, *tant pis*. If France appears to support obviously corrupt and lunatic African dictators, a shrug of the shoulders is what most men in the street would offer as comment. If the President refuses permission to the United States to use French airfields for a strike against Libya, a frisson of satisfaction runs down the spines of most people. De Gaulle restored France's confidence in herself after those terrible decades which saw governments come and go, the fall of France in 1940, the tragedy of French Indochina and Algeria, the debacle of Suez. Pompidou and Mitterrand have maintained the line of independence.

The French are grumblers, but on one point they are united: France is, for all her faults, the best, most civilized, most beautiful country in the world. Is there any need then to travel abroad when there is everything that anyone could possibly want at home? The French are serious sportsmen and serious inspectors of their national heritage. It is all there on their doorstep.

Theodore Zeldin gives some interesting figures for 1929 showing the differences between Britain and France in the number of people traveling abroad:

		BRITISH TRAVELERS	FRENCH TRAVELERS
TO	Switzerland	204,000	104,000
	Italy	132,000	97,000
	France	881,000	—
	England	—	55,000
	Norway	28,000	3,136
	Japan	6,391	883

On the other hand, France had more visitors in the same year than any other country in the world except for Switzerland. They divided up as follows:

FROM	Britain	881,000
	Spain	350,000
	U.S.A.	296,000
	South America	150,000
	Netherlands	55,000
	Switzerland	45,000
	Belgium	38,000
	Germany	35,000
	Austria	30,000
	Other Countries	30,000
	TOTAL	1,910,000

The seeds of this distaste for travel abroad were sown in the nineteenth century. According to Zeldin,

> The timid abbé Hulot—who was worried by every new or old amusement, from dancing to novel-reading—published little books to urge people to stay at home, rather than face the hazards of corruption in public carriages full of strangers: and if you absolutely had to travel, he advised, pretend to be asleep, so as to avoid conversation.* As late as 1878 a travel

* *The abbé's advice on how to avoid bores on trains seems perfectly sound. One wonders, too, whether Jacques Tati, who created in Monsieur Hulot one of the great comic characters of the cinema, had ever read the abbé's little books. He might then never have traveled to the United States.*

guide urged men who ventured on trains alone to arm themselves with a revolver or cane. Some young women long continued to express terror at the idea of travelling by train as
they later feared aeroplanes; some doctors claimed to share
these fears, for they reassured their patients that travel was
not dangerous provided it was endured under medical super-
vision. Commercial travellers had special diets composed for
them because of the troubles their constant movements produced.

Travel, though, is one thing; opinion is something quite different. After 1815, French attitudes toward Britain softened. Voltaire had already written admiringly of British parliamentary democracy. In the nineteenth century, Britain was often held up as
a model of liberalism, and the best counterbalance to the autoc-
racy of Russia and Austria. In 1865, Charles de Rémusat said: "I
confess willingly that the dream of my life has been the English
system of government in French society." At the same time, Hippolyte Taine declared, a trifle overoptimistically, that any boy at
Eton knew more about politics than most French deputies. Taine's
disciple, Emile Boutmy, founded the School of Political Sciences
in Paris, an establishment designed to promote English theory.
Boutmy saw the English and the French very differently, and his
analysis tends toward the cliché. The English, he thought, were
much affected by their damp and misty climate, and were forced to
break out of it with vigorous action and ardent imagination. The
climate of France was quite different, and the French were, consequently, given to clarity of ideas: "These classify themselves auto-
matically in the brain, which enjoys reviewing them, and expressing
them in polysyllabic, joyous and sonorous words, pronounced
slowly in a warm air which carries them back whole to the ear.
Thought and speech are in France naturally analytical; both are
at once a representation of reality and a source of enchantment;
they absorb, like a theatre stage, the successive march, the ordered
deployment of ideas and images; they become in some way part of
the external world."

Boutmy descended into chauvinism when he moved on to the
subject of sex. "Anyone who has lived long in England knows the
bestiality of the majority of the race. Sport, gambling and drunkenness are among the pleasures the English appreciate most. In

sexual relations . . . the Englishman goes to the object of his desires, instead of combining love-making with light entertainment and with the pleasures of conversation. The sensuality of the upper classes is concealed by a heavy hypocrisy . . . the lower classes can amuse themselves only grossly and violently." He might just as well have been writing about his fellow countrymen. Boutmy was provided with a powerful telescope with which to observe England from the safety of his ivory tower. He failed to descend from this tower in order to wander the streets of Paris. Edgar Quinet leveled a far more damaging accusation at England: It was boring. And François Mauriac wrote uncompromisingly in 1937: "I do not understand and I do not like the English, except when they are dead and a thousand commentators, a thousand published letters, intimate diaries, information supplied by Maurois and good translations finally convince me that they are not Martians but brothers." English writers were translated and read, but the only author to achieve real popularity was the novelist Charles Morgan, who purveyed a kind of dreamworld where the pace of life was slow, genteel, and, to English readers, somewhat lackluster.

In many respects, the French have shown far more enthusiasm for the Americans, and the Americans have repaid the compliment. Long-vanished revolutionary fervor, which joined France and the United States in the eighteenth century, was no longer an influence. What many French admired about America was her vigor, her youthfulness, her pursuit of progress. Paul Morand, writing in 1930, was unequivocal in his praise: "I love New York, because it is the largest city in the universe and because it is inhabited by the strongest people in the world, the only one which, since the war, has succeeded in organising itself, the only one which does not live off credit from its past." American writers who flooded to Paris in the 1920s spread the word: Fitzgerald, Gertrude Stein, Hemingway. Gershwin and Cole Porter set their musical comedies in Paris.

Inevitably, there was a backlash. Jean-Jacques Servan-Schreiber, in *Le Défi Américain,* warned of America's industrial and financial takeover of Europe. Disapproval was shown toward the excessive sexuality in American films and novels. In a 1953 opinion poll, the great majority of those questioned professed to a dislike of jazz, Coca-Cola, and American movies. Only 23 percent liked American cigarettes very much. On the other hand, over half agreed that American domestic appliances were a good thing, and only 9 percent disapproved of them.

Many Frenchmen strongly disapprove of the incursions of American slang into the purity of the *langue française*. I have already touched on this aspect of chauvinism, and all that now needs to be done is to list a few words which have been absorbed into French and the dates of their first appearance. "Fashionable" appeared in 1803, "pyjama" in 1837, "baby" in 1850, "cocktail" as early as 1860, "flirt" in 1879, the "grill room" in 1893, the "lavatory" in 1902, and "shorts" in 1933. Franglais has been around for a long time, and the French language is virtually unscathed.

Chauvinism is alive and well in France, just as it is in every country in the world; sometimes it strengthens, more often it weakens. It would be absurd, and damaging, if it did not exist at all. The arts and sciences flourish best in an atmosphere of self-confidence; economic and social improvements are not likely to materialize when a nation has lost her own spirit. France can infuriate her allies and neighbors by her independence of mind. It is a small price to pay for the inner strength which gives birth to that independence.

So France stands convicted of chauvinism, but the sentence handed down is a suspended one. The clichés will continue to be rolled out, some of them accurate images, a few hopelessly adulterated, the majority revealing a blurred effect heightened here, faded there. And the French will continue to apply *their* clichés to everyone else. Major Thompson and the American in Paris have much to answer for.

xiv

Envoi

CAURENCE STERNE summed up the French with these words: "They are a loyal, a gallant, a generous, an ingenious, and good-temper'd people as is under heaven—if they have a fault, they are too *serious.*" It is a fair analysis. The English have rarely been so generous (the Scots, retaining a trace of the Auld Alliance, are kinder). I am an unashamed Francophile, rather like Miss Crawley in *Vanity Fair,* who loved French novels, French cookery, and French wines. When I arrive in France, whether at a Channel port or an international airport, I capitulate, over and over again. The food *is* better, the wine is better too (the novels are not, but one cannot have everything). The country-side is astoundingly beautiful. The palaces and châteaux, country houses and gentilhommières impress and delight. Streets in Paris still look like Utrillo paintings. Like Ford Madox Ford, I expand as the train races southward, the pine trees and cypresses appear, the sun glows.

France possesses unparalleled charm, that evanescent, indefinable characteristic. The landscape has it, the people have it, above all the way of life has it. All this is, of course, foolish exaggeration. Without one's rose-tinted spectacles, it is easy to agree with William Cowper, when he spoke about his own country, England:

> *I would not yet exchange thy sullen skies*
> *And fields without a flow'r, for warmer France*
> *With all her vines.*

And yet . . .

Suggested Readings

THIS IS a list of some books which have given me both pleasure and illumination. I have already mentioned my debt to Theodore Zeldin, whose *France 1848–1945* is brilliantly lucid, finely written, and a compendium of irresistible quotations; for convenience, it has been divided up into five separate paperback volumes, each containing new material. For a work of general history, I would add D. W. Brogan's *The Development of Modern France*. Theodore Zeldin has also published more recently a book entitled simply *The French*. It is hugely enjoyable and informative, though I feel that Dr. Zeldin has been defeated by the intractable problem of conveying the essence of French humor, something I have not dared to attempt.

I have also mentioned my debt to Richard Cobb, that great expert on Simenon, low life in France, and claret. I count him as a friend, and reread his books with mounting pleasure. I would pick out in particular *Promenades*, which he subtitles "A Historian's Appreciation of Modern French Literature" but which ranges far more widely. Other books of general interest, some of which contain more prejudice than sense, include Alain Peyrefitte's *The Trouble with France*, Raymond Rudorff's *The Myth of France*, René Dabernat's *Messieurs les Anglais*, which says just as much about the French as it does about the English, and Jean-Jacques Servan-Schreiber's *Le Défi Américain*. Much more to my taste is Alan Houghton Brodrick's *Cross-Channel,* a beautifully evocative book written out of love. And John Ardagh's books on modern France are essential reading.

Turning to military matters, Alistair Horne's superb trilogy—*The Fall of Paris, The Price of Glory* (on Verdun), and *To Lose a Battle* (on 1940)—is indispensable; I would add his short book *The French Army and Politics 1870–1970.* André Maurois's *Why France Fell,* Edward Spears's *Assignment to Catastrophe,* and Henri Amouroux's *La Vie des Français sous l'Occupation* are interesting.

Travel books worth reading include: M. F. K. Fisher's *Two Towns in Provence,* Ford Madox Ford's *Provence,* E. V. Lucas's *French Leaves,* Henry James's *A Little Tour in France,* Arthur Young's *Travels in France and Italy,* W. Scott's *The Riviera,* A. S. Forrest's *A Tour Through Old Provence,* Tobias Smollett's *Travels Through France and Italy,* Stendhal's *Travels in the South of France,* Hippolyte Taine's *Journeys Through France,* Constantia Maxwell's *The English Traveller in France,* Gertrude Stein's idiosyncratic *Paris France,* and E. M. Hulme's *Wandering in France.*

John Russell's *Paris* is lively and beautifully illustrated. E. V. Lucas's *A Wanderer in Paris* and Mortimer and Dorothy Menpes's *Paris* have period charm, as does Fanny Trollope's *Paris and the Parisians.* Vincent Cronin's *Companion Guide to Paris* is a model guidebook (as are Ian Dunlop's guide to the Ile de France and Archibald Lyall's to the South of France in the same series).

Nicholas Faith's *The Winemasters* is both hilarious and instructive. Hugh Johnson's *Pocket Wine Book* should, *tout court,* be in every sensible person's pocket. The Folio Society does an excellent edition of Alexandre Dumas's *Le Grand Dictionnaire de Cuisine,* which it calls *Dumas on Food.* It is hardly necessary to emphasize the pleasures derived from reading Elizabeth David's various cookery books. Patricia Wells's *Food Lover's Guide to Paris* is pleasantly quirky. Reay Tannahill's *Food in History* is an excellent survey. David Sexton's article in the *Financial Times* of 24 August 1985 on the bottled water industry is well worth looking up.

For history, Lucy Norton's three-volume edition of the *Historical Memoirs* of the Duc de Saint-Simon is superb. See also her *Saint-Simon at Versailles,* Nancy Mitford's *The Sun King,* and Ian Dunlop's *Royal Palaces of France.* Hesketh Pearson's *Henry of Navarre* is not perhaps that writer's most accomplished biography, but it is not to be despised. The Folio Society has done an excellent edition of the Goncourt brothers' *Journal* and a compilation of accounts of the siege of Paris, edited by Joanna Richardson, under the title *Paris Under Siege.* Nicholas Wadley's edition of *Noa Noa: Gauguin's Tahiti* is impeccable. Roger

Nichols's *Ravel* is an ideal introduction to that ideally French composer. Edward Lockspeiser is the expert on Debussy.

I have left Marcel Pagnol to the last. His autobiographical books, translated as *The Days Were Too Short* and *The Time of Secrets*, conjure up the essence of France, though admittedly of only one area, and of growing up more perfectly than any other book I can think of, with the sole exception of Alain-Fournier's *Le Grand Meaulnes*. Even if you ignore all the other books in this haphazard "bibliography," read those.

Index

Campo Formio, battle of, 40
Camus, Albert, 153, 157, 164–66,
192
Candide (Voltaire), 118, 119,
120–21
Cannes, 124, 140–44
Film Festival of, 143–44
Carême, Antonin, 59–61, 63, 64,
66, 72
Carlton hotel, 64
Carlyle, Thomas, 33
Carthusians, monastery of, 127,
128
Casablanca, 70
Castaing, Lucien, 83
Castelnau, General de, 178
Catherine de Medici, 30, 59, 104,
109, 110, 111, 114, 115
Catherine of Siena, Saint, 130
Catholic League, 90
c c (*consommation courante*)
wines, 82
Céline, Louis-Ferdinand, 166
Centre National d'Art
Contemporain Georges
Pompidou, 41–42
Cézanne, Paul, 131
Chaban-Delmas, Jacques, 82
Chabrier, Alexis Emmanuel, 155
Chaligny, Antoine, 40
Châlons-sur-Marne, 93
Chamberlain, Neville, 184–85
Chambord, Château de, 98, 99,
104–7, 108, 109, 115
forest of, 97, 99
Henry James on, 104, 105,
106–7
Champigny, Château de, 116
Champs–Elysées, 42–43
Chanel, Gabrielle, 189
Channel ports, 12, 15–24, 199
Channel Tunnel, 17
Chansons Madécasses
(*Madagascar*) (Ravel), 156
Chanteloup, Château de, 116
Charles I, King of England, 86,
159, 160

Charles II, King of England,
43–44, 86, 159
Charles V, Holy Roman Em-
peror, 106, 109–10
Charles V, King of France, 86,
130
Charles VI, 29, 86
Charles VIII, 109
Charles IX, 86, 88
Charles X, 106
Chasseur Français, Le, 136
Château d'If, 139
châteaux, 12, 96–116, 130, 200
Chaumont, Château de, 98, 112–
113, 115
Henry James on, 112
Chausson, Ernest, 155
Chautemps, Camille, 182
chauvinism, 12, 119, 159, 188,
194–98
la gloire vs., 159, 164
linguistic, 119, 164, 188, 198
sexuality and, 196–97
travel abroad and, 194–96
Voltaire and, 119
chéchias, 150
cheeses, 58, 67
Chenonceaux, Château de, 97,
98, 99, 113–15, 116
Henry James on, 114, 115
Cherbourg, 17
Cher river, 113, 114, 116
Cheverny, Château de, 98, 99,
107–9, 115
forest of, 99
Henry James on, 108–9
Cheverny, Dufort de, 108
Chinon, Château de, 116
Churchill, Winston, 159, 162,
185
cider, 75–76
cidre bouché, 75
Cimetière de Montmartre, 38
cinq à sept, 55
Cisse river, 116
Clarins, 190
Claude de Bretagne, Queen, 102

About the Author

Christopher Sinclair-Stevenson is author of *Inglorious Rebellion,* a history of the Jacobite uprisings of 1708, 1715 and 1719 and *Blood Royal,* a study of England during the reigns of the first four Georges. He lives in London, England.